Idea to Amazon

Release Your Cutting Edge
Strategic Training & How-To Materials plus
Manuscripts in Every Genre & by Any Author

"Jam-packed with resources for my next project, from legal tips, to trusted freelancers, to helpful timelines... Marnie shares it all." Shelley Hitz, Author/Speaker

"What a great book! **eBooks: Idea to Amazon in 14 Days** *includes a straightforward, simple approach to writing an eBook. The steps from paper to publisher are crystal clear. Thank you Marnie!"* Andrea Sharp, Public Speaker

"EBooks are the future of reading and Marnie's book provides clear, concise and easy to follow steps for authors who are serious about getting published. Her step-by-step directions are helping me make my dream of writing a reality. A truly helpful resource." Michelle Reynolds, CEO, Accel365

"A fast-read destined to help many writers get their work in print and on the market in record time." Donna Best, Public Speaker

"Marnie again and again turns vague ideas into concrete action plans, mapping the way from dreams to success. I have no doubt my book will be better because of what I've learned from her. I am excited to use some of the tips on my job as well." Marla Hartson, Project Manager

How to See Your Book on Amazon Fast

eBooks:
Idea to Amazon
in 14 Days

by Leadership Mentor
Marnie Swedberg
www.Marnie.com

eBooks:
Idea to Amazon in 14 Days
Copyright © 2010
by Marnie Swedberg
http://www.marnie.com

Cover Design by Erin Adler
Lauren Graphics, Inc.
erinlaurengraphicsinc.com

All rights reserved.
Published in the United States of America.

Website Links. We apologize in advance for any inconvenience caused by the changing of information outside our control, including the change or removal of linked URLs.

For more information contact:
Gifts of Encouragement, Inc.
Marnie Swedberg
Warroad, MN, USA
877-77-HOW-TO
877-774-6986
http://www.Marnie.com
info@marnie.com

Swedberg, Marnie.
eBooks: Idea to Amazon in 14 Days / by Marnie Swedberg

First Edition/Paperback Book: 2010
ISBN 978-1-450-57229-3
ISBN-10 1450572294

Dedication

23 years to the day after Mark David Swedberg made his debut into the world, this little book debuted on Amazon.com.

I like this new book, but I love my firstborn son. He loves me, enjoys my cooking, introduces me to great authors, shares his dreams with me, cares about mine, and is a great help to me.

So, this book is dedicated to you, Mark, and to everything God is going to do in and through you, both here on earth and for eternity. It is my great honor to call you my son.

Acknowledgements

Dave. Despite subjection to the day-in, day-out rigors of life with Marnie, this remarkable man just keeps on loving me. It's been 26 years and counting. I love you, Dave.

Kari. Thank you for volunteering, going sleepless, and serving me in so many ways. This project could not have happened without Kari Anderson by my side.

Kathleen. Someday, my dear, we may meet. Thanks for *12 Keys to Writing Books That Sell*. Your willingness to write that book made a difference in my life.

VAs. PAs. Freelancers. We did it! We pressed hard, hung together (mostly) and got it done! Thank you for all you did, the way you rushed, and your patience with scattered-brained me. You rock!

Table of Contents

Personal Note from Marnie — 8
Chapter 1. Get Your eBook Published ASAP — 13
Chapter 2. Write for Two Audiences — 22
Chapter 3. Ask the Right Questions — 27
Chapter 4. Keep It Legal — 41
Chapter 5. Add Quotes, Review These Notes — 47
Chapter 6. Super-Edit Your Work — 57
Chapter 7. Break Writer's Block — 61
Appendix I. View the Project Time Line — 73
Appendix II. Write to Sell — 86
Appendix III. Find a Writing Coach — 93
Appendix IV. Research Like a Pro — 96
Appendix V. Meet the eBook Architect — 98
Appendix VI. Format for Handhels & POD — 103
Appendix VII. Create a Cool Cover — 106
Appendix VIII. Get Your ISBN — 109
Appendix IX. Sell Your eBook — 111
Appendix XI. Progress Toward Paperback — 119
Appendix XII. Choose a Paperback Publisher — 123
Appendix XIII. Use Waiver for Long Citations — 148
Appendix XIV. Obtain a www.YourName.com — 151
Appendix XV. Outsource Virtual Assistants — 154
Appendix XVI. Promote Via Blog Tours — 191
Appendix XVII. Prepare for Common Questions — 198
About the Author — 211

Preface
Personal Note from Marnie

Many authors are overwhelmed by the thought of finding a publisher, discouraged by rejection letters, or confused by the long list of self-publication options.

In these pages, I model a journey, showing what it looked like for me to go from concept to Amazon in just 14 days.

While it may take you twice, or ten times, as long as it took me, you need to know that getting published this month or this year is a reasonable goal. You can do it!

Although my first book was published with a big New York publisher, I have been content to self-publish nearly a dozen eBooks, happily selling these how-to guides as downloads from my own websites.

Before January 5, 2010, I had never seriously contemplated publishing my eBooks at Amazon.com or anywhere else, and the thought of writing an eBook on the topic, "How to Write eBooks," was the farthest thing from my mind.

But then the phone rang.

Day 1. Tuesday, Jan 5, 2010. 1:05 PM

I don't recognize the number on caller ID, but I know the voice as soon as I hear it: Barbara Jauquet-Kalinoski, Director of the Northwest Regional Library System, former Oprah guest and long-time personal friend.

Barb invites me to do a 3-day, 7-location pinch hit training program because their original guest cancelled after the promo was published and patron anticipation was already building.

As a pinch hit speaker, I am immediately excited by the ever-so-familiar topic. There is no thought of writing an eBook: I am simply expected to show up and train people on what I know.

I begin preparing immediately.

Within a day, the research results peak my curiosity: much of the information is new to me and the assignment begins to take on the look and feel of a much larger project. In addition to the large pool of unfamiliar practices, the keyword research proves invigorating and I begin to feel my eleventh eBook comin' on.

I toss simplicity to the wind and embark on an insane quest to learn everything I can about the recent changes and opportunities available through eBook publishing, and to share what I uncover with the largest audience possible.

I think, "If I can write and publish an entire eBook before my first presentation, the speech notes will be a piece of cake."

It's a huge challenge: I have less than 14 days to research, write and edit an entire book, a project that usually takes months or years to complete.

Day 12. Saturday, January 16, 2010. 12:40 PM

I am adding the finishing touches to a single-spaced, 103-page manuscript. Not bad! We are on our final edits, and the only thing left is Kindle formatting. Monday morning we publish to the Amazon Kindle Store as an eBook.

My only regret is that we could not grind this through five or ten more rounds of editing. Each time I read a paragraph, I tweak something... and each tweak wreaks havoc with the surrounding content.

Such is the nature of personal publication on a tight deadline. Every business person understands this dilemma.

Day 28. Monday, February 01, 2010. 4:00 PM

The eBook has been in the Amazon Kindle Store for 14 days now and is receiving good reviews. In the interim days, two events launched my add-on challenge:

- My final day of lectures was postponed for two weeks due to bad weather during which time

- I learned that it is possible to take a polished eBook to paperback via Print on Demand (POD) with only a few extra, simple steps.

I went back to work, researching the POD aspect of the process, doing more writing and editing, and I am now reading the final paperback manuscript one last time.

Amazing! This project went from difficult to impossible, and back again. Yet, within 48 hours, we will be ready to print some paperbacks. This is truly a remarkable time in history to be an author.

You Are Invited to Come Along for the Ride

Join me and learn how to prepare and publish a polished manuscript targeting our 2.0 culture and today's publishers.

Hold on to your hat for a rollercoaster ride including actual conversations with my eight outsourcers, shocking discoveries that could make or break your writing career, and all the details it takes to move one idea from embryo to publication in a ridiculously manageable amount of time.

The trip will cost you about two hours. We invested way over 100 for the eBook and closer to 300 for the full paperback version.

Please

Before you publish your book to the Internet, it is critical for you to comprehend that its fate will be in the hands of people who don't know you, don't care about you and aren't shy about telling the world exactly what they think about your book. You need to be prepared.

Here is what you must know before you even consider posting your prize for public review.

- Comprehend the culture and power of 2.0 and how to maximize it as an author.

- Create a cover that builds interest, desire and curiosity.

- Position yourself to attract the attention of a traditional, paying, paperback publisher.

- Stay legal by using proper citations.

- Compete head-on with the best-selling authors by behaving like you already are one.

- Hire experts for $5-150/hour to help you refine your product before you post.

- Format your manuscript with e-readers in mind.

- Move to paperback publication on your own ASAP.

It isn't rocket science, but much of the content contained in this book is very new.

God speed, my soon-to-be-published friend!

Love,
Marnie

PS – I would love it if you would connect with me online at your favorite social networking site. Find me at:

http://www.twitter.com/MentorMarnie
http://www.facebook.com/MentorMarnie
http://www.linkedin.com/in/MarnieSwedberg
http://www.MarnieSwedberg.com – blog
http://www.BlogTalkRadio.com/MarniesFriends - Talk Show

Chapter 1

Get Your eBook Published ASAP

Every author's worst fear is that after investing months or years writing that stellar best seller, no one will want it.

Allen R. Kates is a book editor and best selling author with 30 years of experience. He estimates that the average, 250-page, 6x9" book takes 400 to 700 hours to research and write (1). We put together the 103-page eBook in about 100 hours and the 213-page paperback in just over 300, not including the years it took for all of us to attain the level of expertise we brought to the table.

Writing a book is an enormous undertaking. If you write it, you want people to read it. Unfortunately, many authors invest years and never see one word published.

The Money Factor

As the owner of three businesses, I can tell you from experience that every business, including book publishing companies, has to make money to survive. Businesses can take some risks, but mostly they need sure-fire bets.

In the sphere of publishing, an acquisitions editor needs new authors who have the proven potential to slam in some home runs for the company. In a down economy, publishers cannot afford the long-shot author. It is your job to prove that you are the author they've been hoping to find.

It is my hope and premise, that by getting our books to perform like best sellers on Amazon, we have a shot at attracting the attention of the heavy hitters. We may find that we prefer PRO Authorship (Published Rights Ownership) but it would be fun to have the opportunity of being found and published by an established big brother.

The Beauty of eBook Publication

EBook publication may not be right for you. Stephen King said, "Yes." JK Rowling said, "No." But one thing is for sure: if you decide it is right for you, now is the time to act.

December 25, 2009 marked the first time in history that Amazon.com sold more eBooks than traditional books. January 27, 2010 was the day Apple unveiled the iPad.

These headlines are huge news for unpublished authors.

Right now, any author, including you, can be a published author at Barnes & Noble, Sony Stores and, yes, Amazon, without a publisher and for the price of a weekend vacation.

Amazon.com is one of the busiest websites in the world. If you do it right, people will find your book and buy it. And when they do, it has the same opportunity to be an Amazon best seller as any other book, even those promoted by New York publishers.

The Relevance of Reader Reviews

We live in a 2.0 culture where your online success hinges on social acceptance. 2.0 refers to the interactive nature of online communications including blogs and social networking sites like Twitter and Facebook.

If readers leave glowing comments on your book's sales page, giving it four or five stars, you're in good shape.

But if they feel disappointed, look out! Negative feedback from anyone, even a malicious-drunk or an uninformed reader, can be the kiss of death.

Think Ahead

As you begin writing, or preparing your completed manuscript for publication, always approach your work wearing dual-thinking caps:

- Think like a writer/publisher:
    - You must write, edit, format, upload and market your book on your own without the support of a seasoned editorial team behind you. That's a tall order.

- Think like a book proposal writer:
    - Do everything in your power to make your eBook an attractive sales piece. Could this be a best seller?

If you do not know how to write a book proposal, learn how to before you publish your eBook.

Literary Agent, David Sanford (2) provides the best proposal-writing training document I have ever seen. It is available at http://www.LeadershipAttitudes.com.

The eBook Revolution

eBooks are changing the way customers, authors and publishers do business, opening new doors for unpublished authors.

Trying to get a good book, even a truly great book, published by a big traditional publishing house used to require one of these three things:

1. You needed to know someone in the industry

2. You needed perfect timing: your book proposal had to float across the right desk at the right time in order to be considered or

3. You needed to self-publish in paperback format, hoping to generate enough sales to attract the attention of the big players.

Until recently, there have been only two forms of publication available to authors:

1. Paperback self-publishing companies require you to pay them for the privilege of seeing your book in print.

2. Traditional publishers pay you for the privilege of printing and distributing your work.

Obviously, it is much harder to get the attention of the paying firms.

Thanks to a 2.0 generation, consumed with cultural relevance and reader feedback, a new door for authors is now open.

eBook & POD (Print on Demand) Publishing

From my perspective, eBook- and POD-publishing are both amazing opportunities for unconnected, unpublished authors.

- Both allow you to get your book out there where individuals can purchase and enjoy it

- Both provide a way for you to be "discovered" by agents and acquisition editors from even the biggest publishing companies

- eBooks enable you to connect with the growing population of e-Readers and

- POD offers you the ability to sell and give-away signed copies.

Authors who retain their Published Rights Ownership (PRO Authors), may find that they prefer to remain independent and that's an option.

Financially, these things are now pretty equivalent:

- Fly to New York City and rent a car to meet with a publisher face-to-face (of course, getting the appointment is the hard part).

- Pay to have 50 copies of your book published by a self-publisher in paperback.

Additional, less expensive options include:

- Publish an eBook online so your fans can find, purchase, and promote your work for you.

- Register with a POD publisher and have your book online in a matter of weeks.

EBook- and POD-publication are great ways to get your book out there. Uploading your resources to Amazon adds power to your platform: Google search results frequently show Amazon books and authors near the top of the list.

If your book is done right, as described in the following pages, and your topic answers your audience's burning questions, you are bound to be found.

Writing your book for eBook publication takes you ridiculously close to having a paper-version manuscript ready for POD publication. That final step requires less than a month and is very doable.

Why Publish an eBook When You Can Publish a Paperback?

We are sitting on the tip of an eBook iceberg.

In a May 4, 2009, CBC News article, Fred Langan wrote about his first eBook experience using a handheld reader:

> "I started reading it at an airport and then continued on a plane. Soon I forgot it was an e-book and was into the story. Maybe it's infatuation, but for reading in places like an airport or a plane, the e-book seems easier than the real thing." (3)

Online researcher, Vince Knightly (4), offers three reasons why eBooks are better than paper. Handhelds provide 1) an online dictionary, 2) enough memory space for up to 1,000 books at a time, and 3) a "read-to-me" feature.

When you highlight a word, it shows the definition; if you get bored, you pick a different book; and if your eyes get tired, you select a male or female voice, set the speed of rendition, close your eyes and enjoy an audio book.

Book Oven blogger, Hugh McGuire, writes,

> "I've got an iPod touch, and on it I have recently:

- read a novel at 4:30 AM while suffering from insomnia; previously I would not have been able to do so because I would not have wanted to wake up my wife with the light,

- read a novel in a dark bar waiting for someone (too dark to read a print book) and

- read on a crowded bus (too crowded to manipulate a novel). All these are moments of reading that previously were not available to me." (5)

Many in the publishing industry, including Beverly Slopen (6), a Toronto literary agent, are requesting authors to submit their manuscripts in eBook format because they can scan them in a wink: anywhere, anytime, without paper, without delay.

Nathan Bransford, another literary agent, cites the fact that huge publishers including Harper Collins, Hachette and Simon & Schuster are delaying eBook releases on important titles. His blog post on the topic quoted Carolyn Reidy, CEO of Simon & Schuster as saying,

> "The right place for the e-book is after the hardcover but before the paperback." (7)

This is a game changer. She implies that S&S is now viewing eBooks as a threat to hardcover sales, but on equal footing with paperback sales. Interesting!

Run, Don't Walk, To Your Nearest Writing Project

Your chance at publishing a best seller may be at its peak, even as I type. We don't know how long this window will stay open, but we do know that it is only a matter of time until the publishing industry responds with radical ways to differentiate themselves from individual publishers, like you and me. Their survival depends upon it.

Blogger and writers' advocate, Elise de Bres, says,

> "For me, eBooks are part of now, not the future. Publishers will just have to deal with it and find ways to embrace the eBook. They need to add something extra to it so that there is a clear difference between an eBook and its paper version." (8)

Whether or not you have your sights set on eventual paperback publication, your task right now is to write an eBook to the best of your ability and publish a quality version at Amazon's Kindle Store, Smashwords and any of the e-reader sites.

Your goal is to write with the handheld reader in mind,

- offering crisp, clean and easy-to-read formatting
- featuring fast-paced and interesting content, and
- breaking it up with frequent headings, indented quotes and bulleted lists.

Again, once you have finished creating a stellar eBook, your POD paperback version is within easy reach.

Endnotes

(1) Allen R. Kates. Writing & Publishing. Retrieved January 14, 2010 from Writing & Publishing. Web site: http://www.writingpublishing.com/

(2) David Sanford, Credo Communications. http://www.credocommunications.net/

(3) CBC News - Technology & Science - Latest e-books win over ... (n.d.). Retrieved from http://www.cbc.ca/technology/story/2009/05/04/f-langan-eBook-readers.html?ref=rss

(4) Electronic Book—3 Reasons EBooks Are Better Than Paperbacks. (n.d.). Retrieved from http://ezinearticles.com/?Electronic-Book---3-Reasons-EBooks-Are-Better-Than-Paperbacks&id=3347186

(5) Hugh McGuire: Publishers: Go to the Eyeballs. (n.d.). Retrieved from http://www.huffingtonpost.com/users/logout/?referer=%2Fhugh-mcguire%2Fpublishers-go-to-the-eyeb_b_171786.html

(6) Beverly Slopen, Beverly Slopen Literary Agency. http://www.slopenagency.com/sa/

(7) Books Blogs (French, John, Club, Wordpress) WhatYouKnow.net. (n.d.). Retrieved from http://www.whatyouknow.net/books/blogs.htm

(8) Are eBooks the next generation of pocket books? - Ecademy. (n.d.). Retrieved from http://broadband.ecademy.com/node.php?id=142126

Chapter 2

Write for Two Audiences

It is not enough to write a good book. You must differentiate your book *and yourself* from other experts in your field.

As you write, develop your plan to compete in an overcrowded marketplace:

- Analyze your personal strengths.
- Consider your competition.
- Find out what is missing in the market.
- Determine a direction.
- Develop working chapter headings.
- Research to unearth strong keywords.
- Brainstorm for irresistible title ideas.
- Confirm title availability for the best one.
- Nail down your chapter headings, incorporating as many keywords as possible.
- Make your book a "must read" in your genre.

One of the newest terms is "cooler talk," which refers to excited chatter around the employee water cooler. It's called "buzz," and when it happens for your book, you know you are onto something.

In the middle of this whirlwind writing project, including its super-tight publication deadline, a close friend, Larry, the father of four, was laid off. Dave and I broke away and took Larry and Jenn out to lunch.

Shortly after getting in their SUV, Jenn asked what I'd been working on lately. I did my little elevator speech about the upcoming pinch hit engagements after which Larry asked me to tell him the topic of the eBook.

I answered, "It's a book about how anybody, any author, can now personally publish their own book on Amazon, without a publisher or agent, in as little as 14 days."

Immediately, they began brainstorming out loud the names of all the unpublished authors they knew who could use such a book. Within seconds, their thoughts shifted toward peer-professionals who needed to publish papers in eBook format. Just moments later, they were verbalizing how the information in the book might benefit them personally.

Do not be satisfied if people in your target audience can think of other people who might enjoy your book. Keep working your angle until they show interest on a personal level.

You will know you are on target when your friends or colleagues want to add your book to their own reading lists.

These readers are your first target audience; but you will never win their hearts unless you write for your second audience at the same time.

Super Busy Book Editors

The desk of an editor is piled high, his answering machine overloaded, and his personal time constantly infringed upon.

From this moment forward, remember that your self-published book is going to serve as your attraction package for a future traditional publisher. Your publication becomes, in effect:

- the cover letter (book jacket graphic and Amazon feedback rankings),

- the book proposal (promo and table of contents), and

- the manuscript (the eBook itself).

Your goal is to provide:

- Fascinating material from a unique angle,

- Chapter titles that compel window-shoppers to buy,

- Professional, polished writing that pulls readers all the way through the book,

- Marque-quality graphic art on the cover, and

- Easy accessibility, accomplished the moment you upload it to Amazon.com.

Be ready. Things can move fast.

After completing my first manuscript, I wrote a one-page letter to a St. Martin's Press editor whose name I found in the cover of a book. Within a week, I had a call requesting the full manuscript. Within a month, a contract offer, including a $4000 advance. In 1994 that was a solid, if average, book advance for a first-time author.

My smooth ride from unknown author to St. Martin's Press was a direct result of applying the principles I share in this book. You've got to be determined to do what it takes to make an editor want to publish you or it isn't likely to happen.

Understanding 2.0

As book authors, our immediate challenge is much harder than simply pleasing an editor. We must prepare our manuscripts for the most rabid editors in the world: the general public. These armchair critics are people just like us, who buy books at Amazon.com. Their opinion is important.

We live in a culture of throw-away experts where "Monday Night Quarterbacks" love to point out every mistake pros make. The news media and "talking heads" rip people to shreds without a second thought.

Your book is about to be subjected to the whims of the most fickle, self-gratifying and easily-disappointed audience in the world: the buying public. Before posting your book to Amazon, put it to the test.

Kathleen Krull, former editor with Harper & Row and Raintree, agreed to let me include a few dozen questions that editors ask before purchasing and publishing a book. (See Appendix II.) Ask yourself these hard questions and keep working until your book is ready for the toughest readers. Then, and only then, post your prize for public appraisal.

Be a Team Player: Give a Publisher What She Needs

Again, publishing companies have to make money to survive. Make your book irresistible by thinking like an acquisitions editor.

Editors watch for books that can sell to as many markets as possible. Write your book for your individual, genre readers first, but then, keep working until you find ways to use your content to attract major buyers.

Librarians. Libraries exist to increase literacy and provide research support. Their goal is to make reading materials available to everyone.

Common sense indicates that paper books are not going anywhere soon, but it also appears that handheld readers are creating new demands much faster than imagined.

So, guess who is already promoting literacy by offering e-resources for check out?

Write your book in such a way that every librarian in the country will want to have it in her collection. At present, it is difficult for PRO (Published Rights Ownership) authors to get into libraries. This means that it is our job to create a strong, irresistible demand for our books, until the libraries insist access to them.

Educators. Will school teachers or college professors want to build your book, or a portion of it, into their curriculum? Could it find its way onto reading lists? Tweak it for this audience and tap into another market with millions of potential buyers.

This book, for example, would be a great resource for any teacher. How cool would it be for a class to publish a book of stories, poetry, history reports or whatever, onto Amazon.com? It would make an awesome class project, teach numerous life-skills along the way and be a fundraiser for the class trip. Go figure!

Big Box Stores & Warehouse Clubs. Superstores like Walmart, Sam's and Costco sell a lot of books. According to an editor from one of my earlier projects, they like positive mentions in the books they sell. Note how I have accomplished this here.

Chapter 3

Ask the Right Questions

A few days prior to the phone call that launched this book idea, I was traveling and had a few hours to spare. Guess where I went? I spent nearly three hours in a public library studying the new release titles, subjects, colorful book jackets (front, back and flaps) and their tables of contents.

I love to write, but am too busy to write for pleasure. I write for publication and make that my priority. My content must share what is in my head, and at my fingertips, be packaged appropriately and answer the questions submitted to me by the people who call me "Mentor." If I can answer briefly, I write a blog or article; if the answer is longer, I write an eBook or full-length book.

Study your market relentlessly:

- Which topics are hot right now?
- How are they being addressed?
- What authors are at the top? Why?
- What do readers require? Book jackets are your clue.
- What formats are popular? Like shoes, styles change.
- Of all the new books in your area of expertise, where's the chatter?
- What questions are being asked that are not being answered?

Amazon and other online resources can suffice, but a library is the perfect place for you to scope out your competition. Your potential readers hang out at libraries.

Watch them. How are they choosing which books to check out?

- Do they scan a full chapter or just the back jacket?
- Are they making their selection based on the front cover alone?
- Did the author bio attract their attention?

Try their process yourself. Actually "feel" the challenge faced by your future client's when narrowing down their options. They have many choices.

What will make them choose your book over all the others?

Libraries rock because they have:

- Librarians
- No ringing phones
- Comfortable work spaces
- Computers
- Computer support people
- Books galore

While camping out there, take advantage of the resources to do research on your chosen topic, lay out your chapter titles and add your appendices.

Your Unique Perspective

I definitely have a unique perspective!

I struggled through school, barely graduating from 12th grade. I had no interest in subjecting myself to more "educational torture" in college.

I am not a traditional learner and school was a nightmare for me. But I truly love to learn; I enjoy tackling new challenges and have a blast sharing what I discover with anyone who will listen.

The topics I write about, and the content of my books, are almost always a compilation of lessons learned in my daily life.

In most cases, I am minding my own business, when life throws me a curve ball. It might be a job change, move, new baby, new business, or the need to bring a website up to date with new technology or progress from old-school teleconferences to new-tech, Internet radio talk shows.

Every new experience is both excruciating and delightful for me. At first, I usually feel as though I am drowning.

Here's how it plays out:

- I get thrown into the deep end of some pool (lack of information/experience),
- Thrash my way to the surface (with survival level info),
- Repeat this crazed struggle several times until I learn to dog paddle,
- Make my way to the side of the pool, gaining stroke-skills as I go,
- Decide I want- or need-to stay in the water for a while (sometimes a choice, other times a requirement due to a previous decision or set of circumstances),
- Invest energy learning how to swim (research and practice until polished),

- Give swimming lessons (share what I've learned with others).

This upside-down process is the only way I have ever known how to learn. It's painful, which is what makes it uniquely powerful.

My intense need to breathe has allowed me to uncover many strategic shortcuts missed by more traditional learners.

Jim Edwards and Joe Vitale, co-authors of the eBook titled *How to Write and Publish Your Own eBook in 7 Days* (1), recommend a similar, inverted process. I did not have time to read their entire book, but in their system, they have you write your sales promotion materials first and only after those are completed do you begin to write your book.

I use the same concept, envisioning myself doing media interviews on my subject before writing even the first chapter.

Media Interviews

Having done dozens of print, radio and TV interviews, I am crystal-clear about the results I do and do not want:

- I do want to be a rock-star guest, invited back.
- I do want to be totally comfortable with the topic, an expert.
- I don't want my title or subheadings to lead the interview down a trail I am not prepared to travel.

Do you know how embarrassing it is to get stumped by an obvious question based on the title or chapter titles in your own book?

This happened to me when I turned a great title, *The Air of Prayer*, into a timely title, *Recession PMA: Prayers, Meditations and Affirmations* (2).

The book helps people learn how to keep the economic recession from leading to personal depression and radio interviewers immediately dubbed it, "Recession Antidepressants." Unfortunately, *my* definition of meditation and affirmations was limited to the Christian perspective. As soon as I was interviewed on a main stream show, I found myself completely unprepared for the direction in which the title took us.

Envisioning trouble before it happens allows us to avoid it. More importantly, it insures that readers have their expectations met.

Keep in mind that your book and chapter titles are your advertising. If you get the customer into your chapter, don't let her down. Give her what she wants.

Following are the questions I use to avoid needless confusion. I call this <u>The Marnie Method</u>.

1. What is required of me?
2. Which niche should I target?
3. What steps are involved?
4. Are there any good keywords available for a title?
5. How can I best present the information?
6. Which experts will I quote?
7. What will I do with surprises?

Below is how these questions were answered as this book evolved.

1. What is required of me?

I needed an outline and handouts for my pinch hit engagements on the topic, "How to Write an eBook."

Despite extensive personal experience with the subject matter, I had never taught it. I decided the easiest way for me to provide handouts was to write down my process. As I did, I came to understand that I was writing to meet a need in the market: authors are always asking me for tips on getting published, and this eBook publication option is the newest, most reasonable route. The required outline and handouts would be simple to create once the eBook was written.

2. Which niche should I target?

As my personal assistant, Kari Anderson, finished her first read-through of the manuscript, she said, "I always think of a niche as a cubby that an animal digs into for protection. Am I right?"

Yes! That's just it!

Your niche is your unique angle, approach, or new perspective on a worn out topic. It allows you to delight and inform readers who feel bored with their current options.

"How to Write an eBook" was too general to be a niche and thus evolved the niche word combination of eBooks, Amazon, authors, self-publishing and fast.

3. What steps are involved?

Here we focus on the process itself. Once you know your topic inside and out, you are ready to teach it. Explain each step clearly, helping readers achieve their goal in as few actions and with as little hassle as possible.

You can figure out the required steps like this:

1. Think of as many tasks, requirements or process points as possible.
2. Divide these into logical groupings.
3. Give each group a title. These are your chapters.
4. Rank items either in order of execution or importance. These are your subcategories.
5. Include any necessary but random steps in appendices.
6. Begin your research.

4. What keywords are available for a title?

Your title is critical. Would you have bought this book if it was called, "The Marnie Method to eBook Publication?" Probably not: the word Amazon intrigued you, but the name Marnie would have been meaningless.

Your title needs to "shout" the answer to the WIIFM question: "What's in it for me?"

The key to a great title is to use words that answer your reader's subconscious questions:

- I have an idea for a book, but if I write it, how would it get published?
- Is there a way for me to get my book on Amazon without a publisher?
- Could I publish my manuscript as an eBook? How would I do that?

- Do eBook authors even count as authors?
- I have been selling my eBooks at my site for years. Should I publish it on Amazon?

To find appropriate keywords for your title, use Google's Keyword Tool here: https://adwords.google.com/select/KeywordToolExternal.

By typing in the word, "eBook," I learned that the number one result was the word, "eBooks," with 2.7 million hits last month. That's good. Actually, that's stellar!

Unless you happen to have a whole bunch of people chomping at the bit to buy your book before you publish it, I recommend that you find a niche keyword with at least 20,000 hits per month.

After finding the keyword, "eBooks," I headed over to Amazon to discover which books had already been published with that title. I needed to analyze the book jackets, sales numbers and chapter titles for additional keyword ideas to search.

Amazingly, I found *no* books by that title. The number one ranking search term for "eBook" was still available.

My research immediately took on a feverish pitch as I scouted everywhere I could think of to confirm my findings. To the best of my knowledge, no published work entitled, "eBooks" could be found.

After about an hour of wordsmithing, and just in time for my deadline with my event planner, I landed on the title for the seminars: "eBooks: Your Ticket from Unknown Author to Amazon in Seven Simple Steps." Later in the process, we came up with the title for the book, *eBooks: Idea to Amazon in 14 Days*.

Play with your title idea. Tweak it. Run it by people. Work until your title screams, "Buy Me!" The right keyword-rich title and subtitle will assure your audience that this book will answer their burning questions, respect their time by doing it fast, and yield the results they need.

5. How can I best present the content?

Years ago I read somewhere that *Reader's Digest* attributed its success to using 4th grade-level writing. They wanted their readers to be able to relax and enjoy while they read instead of focusing on comprehension and hard words.

Use the same principle as it applies to your field. If you are writing for PhDs, obviously, you don't want elementary-level language. But, even when writing for doctors, use the easiest reading level that will both gain the respect of your peers and provide them an opportunity to relax and enjoy your writing.

If you want to know the reading level of your work, copy and paste a segment of your writing into an online tester such as Added Bytes http://www.addedbytes.com/code/readability-score/. If you own a website, you can test that content at Juicy Studio http://juicystudio.com/services/readability.php#readintro.

What's In Your Closet?

When I write, I like to think of my content as a closet full of colorful clothes. Each article of clothing has an express purpose—you don't just throw slacks over your head, or a jacket under a blouse. Everything goes onto the body

- in the correct order,
- combined with specific accents,

- to create a unique look,
- to match the requirements of the occasion for which one is dressing.

Just as clothing represents the actual text, the closet represents the writing process as a whole.

- The title is the closet walls.
- The chapter headings are the rod.
- The subtitles are the hangers.
- Your personal knowledge, stories and steps are the articles of clothing.
- The added quotes, lists and researched data are the belts and shoes.
- Publication is the door. Open it now for public access.

If you start with research, your book will tend to be impersonal and institutional. By building the book from the bottom up, you add personal flair and enough color to meet the criteria for a book's success.

6. Which experts will I quote?

I hired outsourcers to help me find experts worth quoting. I gave each researcher a list of topic headings and in a matter of days, they supplied plenty of quotable experts plus additional material to support and accentuate my original content.

Note: If you have time to do your own investigating, take a few minutes to read Vijay's tips in Appendix IV. He is a pro-researcher and taking his advice will improve your results.

The most obvious experts to include in your book are those who

- provide critical content for your readers' understanding of the topic,
- lend credibility to the book, and
- are attainable within your budget of time, contacts and finances.

Once you find an available expert, who has addressed the topic about which you are writing, study the surrounding content for clues. It is amazing how many aspects of a broad topic one can simply overlook until the thought is triggered by a corresponding concept.

Scrutinize your work under a spotlight:

- What steps am I missing?
- What instructions have been glossed over or under-explained?
- What resources are other experts citing that are unfamiliar to me?

As your results broaden your understanding of the bigger picture, your value as an expert increases.

Along the way, different points will remind you of personal stories and experiences you might otherwise have omitted, and the quotes themselves will add invaluable depth, pizzazz and professionalism to your finished product.

7. What should I do with surprises?

Does this step sound odd? Writing a book does not fall into the category of a normal, everyday occurrence. It is a unique adventure full of unexpected challenges, set backs and surprises. Being prepared can make the difference between continuation and cancellation of the project.

When the wind and waves rock your writing boat, don't panic! Most of the nasty shocks in life give little more than a momentary jolt. Until you are sure you've got a ship-sinker, stay calm and keep working.

Local and Foreign Outsourcing

I love working with outsourcers because they enhance my productivity and add color to my life. But sometimes outsourcers are the cause of stress and trauma.

Timothy Ferriss can be attributed credit for the new outsourcing rage. I love his book, *The 4-Hour Workweek (3)*, which, by the way, has been reprinted 40 times already, but was first turned down by 26 editors.

Thanks in part, to Tim, my daily life is enriched by the support of freelancers from the United States and outsourcers from abroad.

My U.S.-based web programmer, Ben Simon, of Ideas2Executables (4), charges standard U.S. rates. My team from India, from Qwiki Soft (5) weighs in at a fraction of that hourly cost.

My producer, Michele Reynolds of Accel365 (6), operates from her home office in Evans, Colorado. She charges typical American wages as well, while her counterparts from other countries charge far less.

Honestly, my default comfort zone would prefer to work with Ben and Michele all the time:

- They speak English as their native tongue, which is huge.
- They share my work ethics, which is rare, even in America.
- They sleep when I do, which is a lovely thing.

- They are worth every penny they charge, which is as it should be.

I simply cannot afford them full-time. I hire them when I can, for upper echelon and intricate tasks, but I work with outsourcers the remainder of the time.

I began outsourcing because I did not have the funds to hire Ben for a major website overhaul. He introduced me to the team I am still using for my big programming projects.

I continue to outsource because it is economically feasible, and it works. I love my outsourcers, but I admit that there are unique challenges due to our language and cultural differences.

Even so, I find most outsourcers to be qualified and hard working individuals with whom I can share my life, my projects and some fun.

An Outsourced Surprise

Before I went to bed one night I made a change at the provider's site. In the morning, I found that my action had prevented the outsourcers from working all night.

We lost a whole night.

It worked out fine in the end, but it sure felt bad in the moment.

Surprises happen. Roll with the waves and ride out your sea-sick feelings. Most storms last longer than we wish, but they never last forever.

End Notes

(1) Edwards, Jim, Vitale, Joe. *How to Write and Publish Your Own eBook in as Little as 7 Days* (2007). Garden City, NY Morgan James Publishing.

(2) Swedberg, Marnie (2009) *Air of Prayer,* republished as *Recession PMA: Prayers, Meditations and Affirmations.* Self-Published eBook.

(3) Ferriss, Timothy. *The 4-Hour Workweek* (2009). Crown; New York, NY.

(4) Ben Simon, Ideas 2 Executables
http://www.ideas2executables.com

(5) Manoj Kumar, Qwikisoft www.qwikisoft.com

(6) Michele Reynolds, Accel365 http://www.accel365.com

Chapter 4

Keep It Legal

I lived next door to a lawyer for eight years, but other than that, the closest thing I can give you to legal advice is the knowledge I've gained through personal research and experience. In the same voice that I share information about how to get published, I share from a lay person's understanding of how to stay out of trouble with the law.

Due Diligence

Although I have several eBooks to my credit, I have never before written one from scratch so fast. My original idea was to create a win-win scenario where I would hire a researcher to find me "free domain" articles to cut and paste into my book, giving credit where credit was due.

I am an expert author with Ezine Articles and people legally reprint my articles in *their* newsletters. There is no cost for this as long as they include the entire bio box. From that information I deduced that I could print articles by *other* authors in *my* book by simply giving them credit: I would write the original content first and then include their articles as "expert advice," offering proper citations. It was brilliant!

But, guess what? My idea was illegal.

Fortunately, I read the fine print before I got too far.

In the short-term, my willingness to read the legalese saved me the cost of researching fees for content I couldn't use. Mid-range, it probably saved the hassle of a lawsuit and, most importantly, in the long term, it might have saved my reputation.

We won't always get it right, and we may even get it desperately wrong, but it shouldn't be because we haven't done everything in our power to stay within the legal boundaries.

The following is not a legal definition, but my own rule of thumb:

- Short quotes may be used in quotation marks if credit is given to the originator.

- Longer quotes need permission unless they are in free domain. You will find a sample Release and Waiver Form for long quotes in Appendix XIII.

Use long quotes sparingly. Not only are usage rights expensive, but getting permission can be time consuming.

As you can imagine, I could not possibly jump through publisher's hoops waiting for multiple responses in time to meet my tight deadlines. I opted to use short quotes and to supplement my content with appendices from a few key experts. This decision shortened the publication process by weeks.

Plagiarism: What You Should Know

The legal definition for plagiarize includes the word "fraud." You behave fraudulently when you misuse:

- something you have copied word-for-word, even just a sentence or a phrase,

- words you have paraphrased very closely,

- statistics gathered or reported by another source, or

- someone else's photos, illustrations, diagrams or charts.

During my research for this project, I fell in love with an amazing little online tool called Essay Rater [http://www.essayrater.com]. I now use it for everything related to self-editing.

One of its features is to flag potential plagiarism, which helps in two ways:

- The editing wizard identifies segments where your text matches something already printed online, letting you know when you are quoting someone else.

- It creates a bibliography citation for you based on the text you have placed between quotation marks and its web-search findings. This alone saves hours and dollars because creating a bibliography from scratch is a lot of work.

Catching plagiarism before it catches you is relatively simple. Most cases of plagiarism can be avoided by:

- acknowledging that the text is not original and providing your readers with the legally acceptable way to find the source,
- requesting permission, and/or
- purchasing rights to use the content.

In an effort to avoid plagiarizing the plagiarism cops, I offer this link to the best resource I could find on the topic. It is an excellent article at a site called Plagiarism. http://www.plagiarism.org/plag_article_what_is_citation.html.

If you have any doubts about your unique situation, please contact someone who has the credentials or power to help you make a legal decision:

- the author of the work you wish to copy,
- the publishing company whose work interests you,
- the Plagiarism website, or
- a copyright lawyer.

Cite It Right

There are two basic ways to include citations:

1. If you use quotes sparingly, provide the required citation notes in the flow of the text (i.e. inside parenthesis like this). Website URL citations should be placed in brackets [like this].

2. When you are quoting extensively, avoid frustrating the reader with the constant interruption generated by such inclusions. Instead, add a notation in the text identifying where to learn more (in the book's bibliography).

Whenever cross referencing another section within your own book, keep the notation in text (such as Appendix II).

Be sure to put quotation marks around direct quotes as shown in the following example:

> Award-winning author of 25 books, Karen Wiesner, gives this sage advice, "The best way to tell whether or not you need to get express permission to use something in an article is to answer the common-sense question: Will this source lose face, promotion and/or potential sales if I don't include their contact information?" (4)

The (#) indicates that details about this quote will be found later in the book.

Beyond Legalities

Using other people's material, with proper citation, provides the following benefits to both you and your audience:

1. It is 2.0-friendly. Today's readers require validation from other experts. They don't trust you unless they feel confident that other people trust you.

2. By quoting experts, your ideas are supported and expanded with added credibility, clarity and conviction.

3. You prove to the world that you have done your homework and are, yourself, a reliable source.

4. You introduce readers to a new connection with whom they can further expand their knowledge or professional interests.

5. You provide the opportunity to distinguish between your voice and that of other professionals in your field. Your creativity, originality and presentation style are clearly showcased when silhouetted against the backdrop of other experts.

6. You make friends, because most people consider it an honor to be quoted in a book.

7. You open the door to ask your new friends to preview your book and give you good feedback for the public to see.

8. By quoting experts, you open the potential for a viral revolution, because many experts already have blogs with large followings. If they even mention your book, it could make a difference.

Chapter 5

Add Quotes, Review These Notes

In January of 2007, one of my paperback books suddenly quit selling. I mean, sales just stopped overnight.

It had been my best selling eBook for two years prior to its paperback publication. Since then, it had been a good little Amazon seller while driving additional traffic to my site for three more years.

People loved that little book and sent me fan mail on a regular basis.

Then, all of a sudden, "Boom!" No more sales.

Since my first book experienced a similar fate, because it was taken out of print by my publisher without any advance notification to me, I wondered if the same sad scenario had gone down with my book titled, *Marnie's Scavenger Hunt Handbook (1)*.

The publisher assured me that the book was still available.

My next thought was that my website promotion page must be jeopardized. But when I checked, it was fine.

Maybe my Google Adwords expired? Did I lose my ranking? What happened? Again, everything at Google seemed in order.

After a while, I made my way to Amazon.com. At first, I couldn't see anything different about my page: the book was still available with copies in stock.

I was scrolling down when the horrifying reality of my situation struck me: in a matter of seven days, the book had received two negative reviews from readers. Since there had never been a comment published at Amazon, positive or negative, these two brief notes crushed book sales, this despite the fact that my email bin was full of positive feedback.

Here is my opinion: the Amazon kiss of death is negative feedback without positive balance.

If a book has several positive comments prior to a negative, these factors change:

1. The nay-sayers are less likely to post. It's hard to stand up against peer pressure.

2. If the book is a strong seller in its niche, like mine was, people dismiss the negative in favor of the positive.

After the fact, however, it is nearly impossible to get anyone to post a glowing report because, again, it's hard to stand up against peer pressure. With two negative posts showing, even readers who had previously sent me glowing emails now hesitated to post a positive comment in public.

The Power of Words

In our 2.0 culture, a PhD has been replaced with PF. If you don't get Positive Feedback, and lots of it, you do not have credibility in your niche regardless of how many letters you have behind your name.

As an author, you must proactively generate positive feedback *before* you publish. This is your protection against readers who enjoy giving negative feedback.

Once you have plenty of positives, relax until you receive a negative. At that point, go out and solicit a few more positives. Keep the sales page balanced in your favor.

Your goal is to get your book into the most hands and handhelds possible. If you cannot keep ahead of the negative feedback, pull a Marnie-move: learn from it and resolve to do better next time.

And, by the way, from this day forward, if you enjoy a book, be sure to post a little note on the Amazon sales page. It is an easy and effective way for you to thank and encourage your favorite author, while helping to insure the longest life possible for his book.

Quote, Quote & Quote Some More

As you may have noticed, quotations from experts pepper the pages of this book. Their input broadens your experience as a reader while developing my logic.

In our 2.0 culture, these quotes serve yet another purpose: they generate positive feedback.

Contact each person you quoted in the book, gifting them with a free copy, and inviting them to provide a comment at Amazon.com.

Another Reason to Add Quotes & Links

How many times have you been reading a book when, due to the content, you were suddenly eager to learn more about tigers, text messaging, or Tiramisu?

EBooks enable you to satisfy that desire in the moment, a critical factor in our "now" culture. Website links throughout your book add value, so include as many as make sense.

Free Press, a Simon & Schuster imprint, released the eBook, *Dumb Money* (2), by Dan Gross. After a time, they published the paper rendition. On April 20, 2009, Reuters' ran a conversation between their writer, Felix Salmon and the author in which Gross is quoted as saying:

> "You can convey a lot more information in a less boring manner with a link." (3)

Links are critical, but many readers will not have access to click them, so don't rely on links to make up for boring writing. Your job is to insure an enjoyable reading experience whether the content is read on a computer screen with quick-linking availability or on a static, printed page.

Indexing Isn't for Cowards

People like to be able to find what they are seeking which is why an index adds value to a book.

Traditional eBooks rarely have an index since they are being read online and are easy to search. However, with the recent changes, making much longer texts now available in electronic format, eBook indexes are coming into vogue.

Including an index is a big decision because it is one of the most labor intensive processes involved in writing a traditional book.

An early editor of mine, Barbara Anderson, called one day and said, "With your permission, I am contracting someone else to do your index. I don't feel any author should be subjected to that torture."

Due to the time limitations for this eBook's publication, I ruled out the inclusion of an index.

If you plan to add an index, speed up the indexing process by highlighting your favorite words in a bright color. This insures that none of your key words are missed due to the indexer's unfamiliarity with your subject.

Time-Saving Templates

I think I must be the "Template Queen." Not really, but I love templates.

My website http://www.IdeasforWomensMinistry.com offers over 30 theme development sets including templates for posters, fliers and tickets.

Templates save time, money, hassle and headaches. They keep you legal and consistent. Building your book-format template before you add your content to saves hours of rework later.

Earma Brown helps small business owners, infopreneurs and writers who want to market effectively online. In her article entitled, "Organize Your eBook for an Easy Read," she addresses the beauty of templates:

> "Every successful non-fiction book, including e-books, have a set structure. Readers enjoy easy-to-read maps to guide them through your book. They love consistency. It is disconcerting and unprofessional if you change formats throughout the book.... Use repeating elements in each chapter. Your readers will love knowing generally what to expect in each chapter and reward you by reading your book from start to finish." (5)

Lance Winslow, the coordinator of World Think Tank, has written several eBooks. He asks,

"Are you considering writing an E-Book? If so you should be using a template that you are comfortable with and fits your style. The Template I use is from Microsoft Office 2007 Templates Online, which I modified using a Thesis Template Style so I can add in the information for research, not everyone will wish to do this, but for the types of stuff that I do, I need it in case someone challenges me on anything, I have a back-up and references in the back." (6)

Pre-Work Saves Time

- Select one font. The Kindle™ defaults to a serif font face from Linotype, called "Caecilia." Most likely your word processing program does not offer that font face, so choose Georgia, Arial or Times New Roman and stick with it throughout the book, including chapter headings and subheadings. Differentiate using font size, italics and text density instead of font face.

- Use the same auto-formatting throughout. Indented lists, like this one, are made when you tab in, type an asterisk (*), a space and then your first point. When you click, "Enter," the next line will begin with an asterisk for your next point. To finish the list, press ENTER twice, or press BACKSPACE to delete the last bullet or number in the list.

- Create your headings as you go for easy formatting later.

- Take advantage of Word's indent feature instead of using tabs. Not only will this simplify your formatting as you work, it will save your final product from having meaningless line breaks.

- Insert page breaks instead of clicking "Enter" numerous times to start a new page. (On your toolbar, select Insert, Break, Page Break.)
- Add your citation endnotes in the process: it takes 60 seconds to copy and paste your resources at the end of each chapter. Add them in the order you cite them, and include every published work, quote, or anything else that could possibly trigger a reader's curiosity or a legal copyright concern. Err on the side of accuracy and save time by adding citations as you go along.

Use proper HTML for links. Start with http:// even if you feel secure with just the www.YourName.com. The goal is for your writing-style to work for every reader.

How Long is Long Enough?

As mentioned earlier, eBooks are now available in any length. Mine range in length from 32 pages to over 200. It's really wide open.

Ethan Evans, advises,

> "At a minimum, 40 pages. Anything less than that is a report. Don't allow yourself to be confused by unsuccessful fools who tell you that 3 pages is an appropriate length for an eBook. What do these people think, that customers are suckers?" (7)

According to eBook coach, Ellen Violette,

> "The best size for an eBook is 80-120 pages. Remember, most people are not going to read your eBook online; they are going to print it out and printing can get expensive. I've written eBooks that were 150 pages and I've heard of people writing 200 page eBooks, but 80-120 is optimal." (8)

Images, Tables, Graphs & Other Special Formatting

Before you add photos, special fonts or unique formatting of any type, including columns, charts, and so on, consider eBook reality.

Many people use their home or office printer to make a hard-copy of an eBook. If it empties their color ink cartridge, it is not a good thing. But even fancy fonts and features can be an expensive idea.

Joshua Tallent of eBook Architects, says,

> "The complexity of a book can have a substantial impact on the difficulty of converting it into eBook formats. We must take into account the type of book, the type of source file, and any complexities in the formatting or file structure." (9)

Don't Stretch Your Luck

In my eBook, *SANE: Social Networking Success in 15 Minutes a Day (10)*, I explain the process I go through to decide how many words any idea can justify. I determine whether to explain my concept as:

- A 140-character Social Networking update
- A 300-500-word blog
- A 1,000-word article
- An eBook of up to 100 pages
- An eBook or paper version of more than 100 pages

EBooks can be any length, but paperbacks of less than 100 pages do not have "spines" so they get lost in bookshelves and many stores will not stock them.

Analysis of your book idea may prove that the idea cannot justify an entire manuscript. Like making a mountain out of a mole hill, it is usually a bad idea to try to make a whole book out of a blog post.

Occasionally a tiny thing, like a social networking ping, can result in a pretty big fling.

- When I posted a note online mentioning that I manage my social networking groups of thousands in about fifteen minutes a day, it led to the eBook, *SANE: Social Networking Success in 15 Minutes a Day*, (10) and

- One day I invited friends to my upcoming interview with "million miler," Dan Poynter, which generated chatter enough to lead to the creation of http://www.TheMillionMileClub.com.

End Notes

(1) Swedberg, M. (2004). *Marnie's Scavenger Hunt Handbook Over 50 Extremely Fun and Easy to Run Relationship Building Hunts*. Baltimore: PublishAmerica.

(2) Gross, Daniel. *Dumb Money* (2004). Glencoe, IL. Free Press.

(3) 300,000 Kindle 2's Sold To Date (n.d.). Retrieved from http://www.techcrunch.com/2009/04/16/300000-Kindle-2s-sold-to-date/

(4) Plagiarized? (n.d.). Retrieved from http://www.inforesourcecenter.com/writeway/plag.html

(5) Passion to Profit EBooks & More. (n.d.). Retrieved from http://www.clickeasyeBooks.com/ezine-8.htm

(6) Just Answers - Writing and Speaking. (n.d.). Retrieved from http://www.justanswers.org.ua/articles/135_4.html

(7) How Many Pages Long Should Your eBook Be So That Customers Feel They God Their Moneys Worth? (n.d.). Retrieved from http://ezinearticles.com/?How-Many-Pages-Long-Should-Your-eBook-Be-So-That-Customers-Feel-They-Got-Their-Moneys-Worth?&id=2572870

(8) The E-Book Coach. Frequently Asked Questions. (n.d.). Retrieved from http://theeBookcoach.com/faqs.html

(9) eBook Architects - eBook Conversion Services. (n.d.). Retrieved from http://eBookarchitects.com/conversions/services.php

(10) Swedberg, M. (2009). *SANE: Social Networking Success in 15 Minutes a Day*. Warroad, MN: Self-Published eBook.

Chapter 6

Super-Edit Your Work

Every word matters: even if your goal is to publish your eBook for family and friends, understand that once you publish it, anyone can buy it and pass it along to a friend. Who knows? They might be an agent, editor or publisher. Your reputation is at stake.

The Giant Eyeball

After watching me do a cooking segment on TV one day, a test-kitchen employee for Betty Crocker stopped by my table at a local bookstore. While I was signing the copy she'd brought with her, she said, "I've read your book. I love it. It only had three typos."

That book had been put through the paces by a big publisher, yet three typos survived to remind us we are human.

Before I submitted the manuscript, I had invested eighteen months writing it. In addition, six people had edited it, including an English teacher, a newspaper editor, a science columnist, and a home economist.

That pre-work got me in the door.

Imagine my shock when the first edited version was returned to me covered in red. I learned that an editor's red is a good thing.

To be honest, if I had one more day, week or month before target release of this book, I would invest it into more editing.

Readers will spot grammatical errors you didn't know existed, zoom in on stupid sentence structure and unravel your best attempts at overall organization. Experts in your field will notice holes in your logic and rip it to shreds.

A good editor is invaluable.

Key Editing Concepts

Start with self-editing. Here are a few things to take into consideration:

- Redundancy: Have you shared the same concept more than once? If so, did you note the previous mention?

- Order: Does the content work as arranged? Would a different flow help the reader?

- Balance: Do your chapters feel equally weighted? Have you combined or broken down extremes?

- Patterns: Have you maintained a clear pattern throughout? If most of your chapter titles begin with a verb, all of them need to match. If most chapters begin with a quote, retain consistency.

- Citations: Decide how to notate your citations and where to put your reference notes. Always do it the same way.

Hire What You Need: Editing Terminology

Is your nickname "the Comma Queen?" Do appositives and restrictive functions confuse you? Hire an editor.

People talk, you know. If your eBook is riddled with sluggish writing, grammatical errors, improper use of punctuation or style issues, you are going to get bad reviews on- and off-line.

The following categories provide an overview of the different types of editors I was able to find online. Decide which types of editing your book needs and then proceed to hire good help.

- Proofreaders identify and correct typos, punctuation, misspelled words and inconsistencies in formatting. Much of this can be accomplished with an online editing tool as was described earlier.

- Copy Editors proof for all of the above plus identify errors in capitalization, word usage and tone.

- Full Scale Editors, sometimes called Hard, Heavy, Developmental or Substantive, edit for overall congruity. They report on readability, believability and consistency, noting red flags, unnecessary repetition, cumbersome phraseology and other writing death-traps.

- Formatting Editors tackle the nuts and bolts like page margins, line spacing, indentations, endnotes, heading sizes, references and citations.

- Technical Editors are fact-checkers, whistle blowers and the ones who can spot an exaggeration a mile away. They test everything from recipes to computer codes so readers do not get stuck with a failure when attempting a described process.

There are good editors out there; most are very expensive. But money isn't everything. One of my editors for this book, a college student named Nicole, did a fantastic job for a fraction of what her freelance counterparts charge.

My advice is to flow your work through an online, instant-editor first, then have friends edit it. After you make the appropriate changes, run it through an online editor one last time and then pay a few pros to polish it up.

Chapter 7

Break Writer's Block

The best editor in the world cannot improve your unwritten words.

When you touch your toe to the water of eBook self-publishing, all of your fears, self-doubts and insecurities can easily drown any possibility of success, unless you deal with them head-on.

Even after writing for years, and having been published by some of the biggest and best, I still struggle with fearful feelings. In fact, just prior to getting the pinch hit call and launching this writing project, I'd hit another one of my "Marnie blocks" regarding my writing skills.

As a staff writer for Live Magazine (1), I submit a monthly article into the black hole of my editor's email bin. Sometimes they publish my article, other times not.

A few days ago, I sent my editor, Lorraine Williams, a note because I feared she secretly wished I would resign. One day later, on January 6, 2010, she sent this heartwarming response, used here with her permission:

"I just finished reading your February submission entitled 'Wake Up' and I thoroughly enjoyed it! I have to say this isn't the first time I read your column and a smile has come across my face. I believe you have the heart of the magazine and your articles always express a gentle prompting to the reader to do better and to reach for the Victorious way of living.

"Thank you for sharing your gift with the magazine and our readers. I look forward to reading many more of your columns."

Whew! I was so relieved.

Receiving words of encouragement and directional clarification are the cornerstones of any writer's progress. Unless you plan to write for bears, you should not hide your writing in a cave. Keep asking for input even if you are confident that your work rivals Gone with the Wind.

Zero Distraction

When I write, I postpone every activity that could block the free-flow of thoughts. I follow-up with evaluation, fact checking, data collection and the gathering of suitable stories and illustrations; but while I am writing, none of these things infringe on my space.

During the evolution of this resource, for example, I began by doing enough research to establish the chapter titles. Next, I fleshed out each chapter with subheadings. After that I free-flowed the content of each subtitle, as best I could, and finally, I gathered the statistics and quotes required to either build my case or change my perspective.

Writing Coach

There is something uniquely valuable about personal coaching or joining a coaching group. This may be especially true for those of us who do not write full-time. As an entrepreneur and part-time writer, I need all the help I can get.

I have never had a "writing coach" exactly, but I have hired business coaches whose advice improved my life.

- Thanks to Linda Lopeke (2), my main website at http://www.marnie.com went from confusing to focused; from average to clearly exceptional.

- Thanks to Rick Cooper (3), I overcame my staunch resistance to the social networking craze and am now reaping the benefits on many levels. Join me now at Twitter [http://www.twitter.com/mentormarnie], FaceBook [http://www.faceBook.com/mentormarnie] or LinkedIn [http://www.linkedin/in/marnieswedberg].

My personal coaches have done more for my perspective in one hour than I could have accomplished on my own in a year.

International marketing and book coach, Joan Clout-Kruse, understands the time crunch facing busy people whose writing must occur between other life responsibilities. She writes:

> "I find that writing a book is a big challenge for entrepreneurs. They have no time, no strategic plan, and are struggling especially when writing their first book. They are busy building a business and they need help writing a book because they know how important it is to have an expert book." (4)

If you find yourself feeling discouraged, hopeless or just plain "stuck," consider hiring a writing coach. A coach will help you assess your current situation, clarify your goals, reduce the project to manageable, bite-sized pieces, hold you accountable and provide you with the specific shortcuts that could radically change the turn-around time on your project.

The Best Coach

God is the ultimate writing- and life-coach. He is and has the answer for everything. Just this morning I was flat on my face on the floor asking for His help.

Usually I find that God uses people to answer my prayers.

- My husband loves and balances me.

- My kids and other family members cheer me on and help me succeed.

- Family and friends counsel and encourage me.

- Employees show up every day, work hard, and provide helpful input.

- Personal assistants volunteer their time.

- Virtual assistants and freelance providers work hard and offer feedback.

- Book authors publish their own experiences and research for my benefit.

- The Internet offers great advice from people I respect.

However, even after exhausting all of the above resources, sometimes I am still stuck. My practice is to hire a trusted coach anytime I face one of these three scenarios:

- I know what needs to get done, but can't figure out exactly how to do it.

- I know what to do, am doing it, but keep hitting a brick wall.

- I know what to do, but can't get myself to do it consistently.

Coaching the Group

In my early 30's, people began seeking my advice about their ideas or challenges. I began to realize that I had been gifted with unique abilities and perspectives. Simultaneously, I understood that being a coach as a career, was not a perfect fit for my kite-like personality.

Over time, I developed Coaching the Group (CG) an example of which you are experiencing right now. I can only be in one place at a time. Books allow me to share my life, experience, research and perspective with thousands.

The CG mentality looks like this:

1. Live. Go through your life with an engaged mind, noticing what is being done well and what's being omitted or done poorly.

2. Discover. Research, ask questions and experiment until you discover better ways to accomplish any task of interest to you personally.

3. Share. Make your findings available for the benefit of others in a format that is affordable and accessible.

eBooks: Idea to Amazon in 14 Days, the reading experience you are engaged in right now, is a prime example of CG concepts in action.

For years I learned about writing eBooks, and used what I discovered to publish ten of them. I studied, interviewed experts and put into practice what I learned. But the motivation to invest time, money and sleepless nights did not surface until I was asked to train other people on the topic.

I encourage you to stay alert for similar opportunities. You and your perspectives are unique. When you see a hole in the market with your name on it, do not let roadblocks or discouragements prevent you from sharing what you know with the rest of us who need that information.

If you get stuck, hire a coach. A list of writing coaches is available in Appendix III.

Join a Writing Group

Many writers claim that their writing careers would have been short-lived without the support provided by other writers. The extent of my personal experience with writing groups includes having spoken at some. Thus, I am including numerous quotations in this section, hoping to encourage you to pursue locating one in your area.

John Neeb, a freelance writer and active writers' group participant, says it best:

> "Joining a writers group is an absolute must if you enjoy writing, and even more so if your dreams are to become published one day. It applies a time constraint to keep you moving forward in the craft. You will find help editing your works and develop stronger writing skills. And joining the community will only increase confidence in your identity as a writer. So if you haven't already, take one of the smartest steps possible for your writing journey and find a writers group to join today!" (5)

Greg Knollenberg is the CEO of Writers Write, Inc. He encourages writers to start by defining their goals:

> "Are you looking to meet other writers, have your work commented upon, learn about a particular genre? Are you looking to meet locals or writers from across the nation or the world? If you are beginner, you may not meet the membership requirements for all groups, but you can at least find out what you will need to accomplish to become a member.... When you find the right group for you, it will be well-worth your time and your money." (6)

Beyond critiques and camaraderie, Chicago freelance writer, Janina Rusiecki-Williams, found her new writers' group provided more than she had hoped:

> "In our first meeting, we had a discussion about submitting work to selected literary journals. I mentioned how I was going to sign up for Writer's Market online. And that's when somebody in the group chimed in and told me about a site called http://www.duotrope.com/, which not only gives you masthead information for a plethora of publications, but also has a section where you can track where you have sent your work. And the best part is that it's free. As writers, you know how invaluable this information is. If I weren't a part of my writing group, I'm afraid that I may have never known this." (7)

But not all groups are created equal. Lisa Brunel of Learn to Write a Children's Book gives this sage advice:

> "When you are considering joining a writers group, you would want to be sure that the group has a writing goal for each meeting. Each writer should

> always bring a piece to discuss at each meeting. A new writer should also make sure that there is an interest in their type of writing at these groups.... Keep in mind that it is also a good idea to see if there are guidelines for behavior. Sometimes writers groups can get rowdy, a good writer will have extreme passion for their story, which is why some writers do not like writers' groups." (8)

The next piece of advice comes from Gurmeet Mattu, who has been writing for over 25 years for print, radio, theatre and TV. He is a trained journalist and is best known as a dramatist and comedy writer, having written an award-winning screenplay. He currently resides in the UK. He cautions:

> "Writing groups, whether online or local, are strange beasts and should be approached with caution by the novice writer. The danger lies in the reaction your work gets from your fellow members.... The only thing a fellow novice writer is qualified to comment on is on their own reaction to a piece. An editor or publisher, on the other hand, looks at a piece of text from a commercial angle, to assess what value this piece brings to their organization." (9)

Rebecca Lake is a freelance writer for a number of online venues, including Demand Media and Content Divas. I loved her encouragement to writers and thought it would be a wonderful way to end this section:

> "The writing life is not an easy one and for those whom it chooses, the road can often be long and difficult to navigate. Joining a network of writers can make the trip less confusing and can offer a writer the support they need to excel at their craft. Every writer questions whether the writing life is right for

them at one point or another. It is at this moment that the writing network can make the difference between failure and success." (10)

Start a Writer's Club

If you can't find a club in your area, why not start one?

Joyce Heiser is one of my Leadership Club members over at http://www.marnie.com. The day before I got the call to do the pinch hit training, we "just so happened" to start an email conversation. It came up that she and her friend, Lois, had started a writers group a few years back.

Upon learning of my upcoming training, she sent me a training hand-out she had previously created and gave me permission to recap the main points below for you.

Excerpts from Joyce's training handout:

1. Choose a date and time. We decided on a Saturday morning, since many people don't want to go out again after a tiring day at work. By ending at noon, they had the rest of the day free.

2. Find a meeting place. Our main criterion was "free." We estimated how many we might have, and made a list of room requirements. Since we wanted to serve coffee and refreshments, we needed a kitchen/kitchenette and counter space and/or a serving table. We also needed two tables--one for the speaker and one to display her books for sale. We called several local churches, the library, and the park district, but because of the short lead-time, nothing was available. Then Lois remembered that the community center had rooms. For a refundable

$20 fee if we cleaned up after the meeting, it was available that morning, so we booked it.

3. Find and book a guest speaker. Here again, we wanted someone who wouldn't charge, so Lois asked an award-winning author and speaker friend. As the co-founder of a 19-year-old writing group, Beth was qualified to speak on "How to Grow a Healthy Writers' Group." She came for gas money.

4. Choose a theme. All our advertising focused on the theme of coming to help start a Christian writers group that would gather for education, encouragement and fellowship.

5. Advertise, advertise, advertise. We focused most of our time and energy on advertising. We utilized the local newspapers, Christian radio, bulletin boards, fliers, the internet, and word of mouth. Being in a rural farming area, we knew we might draw from a 50 to 75 mile radius. We did an internet search for community newspapers within that area and sent a press release to each. In addition to the meeting date, time and place, it included names of two contact people, giving both phone numbers and e-mail addresses. We were contacted both ways. We sent an announcement to our local Christian radio station. The meeting was not only announced during the morning community calendar program, but sporadically during the day for two weeks before the meeting. The Upcoming Events Calendar section of the station's website also listed it. I posted the info to two Christian internet writing groups I belong to. Those brought an unexpected response from a lady in Ohio. Her former pastor's wife is a writer. They now serve a church in our area, so the lady sent her name and phone number. We made fliers. Stacks

were left at libraries. We posted them on bulletin boards in restaurants, grocery stores, laundromats, at business establishments and anywhere we saw a bulletin board. Both of us knew local writers, so we called to share the news of the start-up meeting.

In the year and a half since that initial meeting, God answered our prayers for Lighthouse Christian Writers. We have 10 members and are a close knit group who support and encourage each other in our writing endeavors and personal lives. Strong friendships have formed. We send prayer requests through the group and have seen God answer in miraculous ways such as an all day writer's workshop to celebrate our first anniversary.

If God can do this in the rural farming communities of northeast Wisconsin, He can do it in your area...no matter how large or small. Decide now to step out in faith and do it!

Note: Joyce has since moved to South Dakota and is now a member of the Congregation of Christian Writers in Sioux Falls. She is the co-founder of Lighthouse Christian Writers. (11)

End Notes

(1) Live Magazine: Live In Victory.
http://www.liveinvictory.org/

(2) Linda Lopeke, Smart Start Coach.
http://www.smartstartcoach.com/

(3) Rick Cooper, PDA Pro.
http://rickcooper.typepad.com/about.html

(4) Terrific Book Writing Tips and Coach Joan Provide Help... (n.d.). Retrieved from http://www.powerhousewriting.com/index.html

(5) Joining a Writers Group - A Key Step in Your Writing Journey. (n.d.). Retrieved from http://ezinearticles.com/?Joining-a-Writers-Group---A-Key-Step-in-Your-Writing-Journey&id=3136133

(6) Writers' Groups -- Are They Worth Your Time and Money... (n.d.). Retrieved from http://www.writerswrite.com/journal/sept97/gak2.htm

(7) How joining a writing group will improve your motivation to... (n.d.). Retrieved from http://www.helium.com/items/344749-how-joining-a-writers-group-will-improve-your-motivation-to-write

(8) Learn to Write: Join a Writers Group! (n.d.). Retrieved from http://www.articlebliss.com/Art/340742/82/Learn-to-Write-Join-a-Writers-Group.html

(9) Reviewing Articles on ArticleSlash.net, free Articles about... (n.d.). Retrieved from http://www.articleslash.net/t-reviewing.1.html

(10) The Lonely Writer: Benefits of a Writer's Group: Why a... (n.d.). Retrieved from http://writernetworks.suite101.com/article.cfm/the_lonely_writer

(12) Lighthouse Christian Writers. [http://www.mychristiansite.com/ministries/lhchristianwriters]

Appendix I

View the Project Time Line

My inspiration for creating this time line came from a practice I adopted after my 90-year old grandmother, Marie Colwill, was featured in the book, *This Day in the Life Diaries from Women Across America*(1). Since reading that book, I have occasionally captured a day by logging every activity from morning 'til night, just for fun.

Ironically, just a few months before beginning this writing project, I started writing a different book. I think the title will be, *Super Busy: How to Escape Survival Mode*. This is not a 14-day project. I hope to see it published in 2011.

On a random weekday, I logged every single thing I did from the time of first conscious awareness until the time I went to sleep. The diary contains 108 unique "change of activity" entries covering the entire breadth and span of my daily life. The book will include the strategic shortcuts, mental paradigms and spiritual support that enable me to lead a "joy-full" life. My hope is that busy people everywhere will read it and find a way out of the "just do it" trap that saps the ecstasy out of life.

A Facebook conversation a week ago went like this:

> Beth: Marnie, you seem like you never get tired.
>
> Marnie: What?! Of course I get tired... real tired. Then I rest. Then I'm not so tired.

My basic definition of balance is to work and then rest; and then work and rest again.

Sometimes work feels like a walk around the block. This project felt like a triathlon, not that I know what *that* feels like.

During super busy seasons, like the one I am about to describe, I have very little time for any type of rest other than sleep. At times the pressure gets so intense I must focus as if in the labor of childbirth. One time, I couldn't speak to the people around me for nearly a day as I forged through the final stages of a massive launch.

I'm getting better at maneuvering through extreme projects. For example, this time I was able to take both Sundays off, take a Monday trip with my husband and son, Mark, and spend a leisurely lunch with friends. I played the piano and sang, hung out with my family, worked on a puzzle and maintained a presence at both the restaurant and retail store.

This has been the biggest and most challenging race of my life so far. I have thoroughly enjoyed the process and I want you to know that you, too, can enjoy the super busy seasons of your life.

The following is a blow-by-blow rendition of this project's timeline. Enjoy.

5-Jan-2010

Cell Phone. Barbara Jauquet-Kalinoski, Director of the Northwest Regional Library System, calls because she needs a pinch hit presenter. Her pre-scheduled trainer cancelled after the publicity was out and excitement generated. It is a 3-day, 7-location training tour on the topic, "How to Write an eBook." Launch time: 16 days.

Confirm. "How to Write an eBook," their topic, is within my sphere of expertise, the engagement itself, timing, and topic instantly excite me and I am able to find staff to cover my responsibilities at the restaurant, retail store, espresso café and websites while I prepare and travel.

Husband. Float the proposal past Dave who has no red flags.

Producer. Contact Michele to bring her into the loop.

Proposal. Determine to accept the engagement pending detail arrangement. Email the planner my contract proposal.

6-Jan-2010

Details. Receive email including itinerary, remuneration and contract confirmation.

Publicity. Exchange calls with their PR people and program coordinators.

Research. Copy and paste the tables of contents from the best selling books in this category into a Word.doc, seeking both critical and unique angles.

Brainstorm. Select my working chapter titles and subtitles.

Files. Create one file per chapter title into which all research content on that topic will flow.

Visuals. Determine to use handouts vs. PowerPoint slides.

Idea. Deduce that by the time I create the content to create the headings for the handouts, I might as well write an eBook on how to efficiently write eBooks.

7-Jan-2010

Research. Continue to research chapter content ideas.

Keywords. Determine the title and chapter headings based on keyword results.

Solidification. While doing keyword research, stumble upon the fact that Google's number one search term in the niche, "eBooks," is available as a book title.

Subtitle. Formulate the books working subtitle.

Deadline. Set the goal of having the completed eBook published into the Amazon Kindle Store prior to the first day of training.

Team Development. Begin hiring individual outsourcers to help me accomplish my goal.

8-Jan-2010

Team Management. Spend much time each day from here on out hiring and/or providing direction to outsourcers.

Cover. Hire a graphic artist.

Editor. Tentatively select a main editor, reserve her time for Friday, Jan 15.

Template. Create the manuscript template.

Begin Writing. Between interruptions, start to add my ideas, experiences and stories randomly, typing thoughts and entire segments into whatever section seems appropriate.

Permissions. Send email requests to various experts seeking permission to quote longer segments of their work.

9-Jan-2010

Writing. 4:30 AM. It's quiet at this time of day. Make good progress.

Authors. Receive email response from Kathleen Krull with provisionary consent.

Interruptions. Juggle phone calls from restaurant and retail store and answer the doorbell repeatedly. Both of my college-age kids have junkers-for-sale on our front yard and people keeping stopping to ask questions and test drive them. I research and write every spare minute.

Outsourcers. Continue to maintain close contact.

Self-Editing. Register with EssayRater.com

ISBN. Realize my need to order the books ISBN. A horrifying reality: last time I'd checked getting an ISBN took 6 weeks.

Restaurant. 2:45 PM. Sign off to work at the restaurant from 3 PM until close.

10-Jan-2010

Rest. Enjoy worship at Woodland Bible Church, a relaxing lunch out with Dave, Mark and Tim, a delicious two-hour nap, alone-time with God, and a long phone conversation with my daughter, Keren.

Back At It. 8:30 PM. Resume work: research, write and email outsourcers.

Publicity. Determine to launch the eBook marketing campaign during February, which is "Library Lover's" and "National Time Management" Month. Notify my producer to book radio interviews for this campaign, limiting my availability to the week of Feb 22-26, which is "Read Me Week." Perfect.

Decisions. I am now convinced that I have the right editor, but am uncomfortable with my Kindle expert. Continue researching alternative providers.

11-Jan-2010

Goals. 4:23 AM. Realize I must finish adding personal content today.

Kindle™. Select Joshua Tallent as my formatting- and upload-expert. Ask him to provide an appendix for the eBook.

Confident. Calculate that by the time we add quotes, links, forgotten concepts and final formatting, the book will be at least 100 pages, which is long enough.

Blog Blast. Determine to use the popular "blog tour" concept, but to "pull a Marnie" by hosting it all in one week, instead of over a longer period. Hire an outsourcer to research details and book February 22-26 for the Blog Blast to correspond with my media availability.

Travel. 8:30 AM. Dave, Mark and I leave on a 280 mile round-trip during which I mostly ignore the project except for taking one call from the graphic artist.

Home. 7:45 PM. Arrive home to an email bin full of work. One researcher is failing. Consider my options.

12-Jan-2010

Computer. 4:30 AM. Gosh, it's early, but I'm wide awake.

Mistakes. Find and fix a mistake that held up the outsourcers for several hours.

Write. Work on segments that require focused attention before the family rises and the phones begin to ring.

Business Ownership. 8:30 AM. Receive calls from both employees who are scheduled to open the retail store, each needing to take a sick child to the doctor. Drop everything. Get ready to go.

Calls. 10 AM. Back in the office. Pause frequently to take calls from the restaurant, retail store, and US outsourcers and freelancers.

Expert. 11 AM. Conference call with Joshua, the Kindle formatter to nail down details of the job. He agrees to provide the content for an appendix within two days. Awesome!

Lunch. 12:30 PM. Got picked up at the office to have lunch with Dave and friends.

Final Draft. 3:23 PM. Receive book jacket final draft. Only four revisions. Very pleased!

Polish. 7-9 PM. Finish a very rough, first draft. Many "XX"s (which indicate missing content). Send research requests to outsourcers who will start work shortly and work all night while I sleep.

Exhaustion. 9 PM. Exhausted. Go to bed.

13-Jan-2010

Early. 3 AM. Wake up wondering if researchers were progressing or if they needed anything. Decide to get up and find out. Answer two questions and go back to bed.

Hire. 4 AM. Hire three "brainstorming" outsourcers to help me come up with stronger chapter titles.

Excited. 7:35 AM. Sweet! Combine the files and do my first total read-through. The thing has potential! Feeling calm. Knowing this is doable with a lot of help from my friends.

Kari. 9:45 AM My volunteer PA, arrives to begin assembling every conversation between me and the outsourcers for Appendix XX.

Discovery. 1:15 PM. Discover that Essay Rater is automatically building the bibliography. Excited! This is a huge time- and money-saver.

Nap. 2:15 PM. Rest on my bed for 15 minutes.

Pizza, Tacos & Subs. 2:45 PM. Leave for the restaurant where I will work the night shift because one of our gals is out for a medical emergency.

Bed. 10:45 PM. Go to bed.

14-Jan-2010

Husband. 4:12 AM. Dave joins me for a half-hour chat, than goes back to bed while I begin my final major edit of the eBook.

Backwards. I start at the back of the eBook and work my way toward the front, fixing any glitches I meet along the way.

Break. 10 AM. In moving some papers, I find myself holding the sheet music to, "The Blessing" by John Walter and Troy Denning (2). Start playing the piano and Nicole joins in as we sing, "Let it be said of us, that we lived to be a blessing for life." This is my prayer.

15-Jan-2010

Eyes. 4:15 AM. Working in good lighting, but my eyes still complain.

Yikes. 6:30 AM. Editing is taking far longer than hoped.

Arghh. 7 AM. Internet is down. Decide to keep editing.

UhOh. 9:15 AM. Where's Kari? Call her. She misunderstood; will try to find a sitter now.

Terror. 9:55 AM. I am way behind, I cannot access the Internet to touch base with the outsourcers and I don't have phone numbers unless I get Internet access. I am toast.

Down Girl. 9:57 AM. Agitation consumes me, so I walk to my bedroom, lay facedown on the floor, and say "Hi, God."

I thank Him for all the help so far, remind myself and Him that it is not my project, and that if I don't complete it, it's no big deal, and then I ask for help. I stay, lay and pray a bit, resting in His care and praying for everyone involved.

Rock 'n Roll. 10:02 AM. The Internet is up. All I did was take a break to pray and now it's obvious I need to resume work.

Next Surprise. 10:04 AM. Read my editor's email indicating she is *not* going to be able to start editing until this afternoon. Realize that four hours ago, this would have terrified me. But just now, being hideously behind on my part of the editing, I am only grateful. I have time to finish, maybe.

Shit? 10:33 AM. Answer a call for my son, Mark. Explain to the telemarketer he no longer lives here. Hear the reply, "Shit!" Just FYI: When adding icky words to your manuscript, think of people like me. I hate icky words. I feel slapped. Unless you are sure your audience likes to be slapped, avoid using colorful language in your published works.

Help Arrives. 10:40 AM. Kari begins typing the remaining outsourcer communiqués.

Amazed. 2:03 PM. Attach the edited document and press send. Now it's in Nicole's hands.

Truffles. 2:15 PM Dave stops by with some Lindt truffles. Now I can honestly say that I sat around eating truffles today. How funny is that?!

Taxes. 2:30 PM. It is January 15th which means payroll taxes are due today. I stop writing, close all screens, open QuickBooks, and call the restaurant where Kim and I share news before I ask her to bring me food (a 7" BLT baked salad, my fav) and all the bills I need to pay today.

16-Jan-2010

Final Edits. 2:30 AM. Begin going through the edits just submitted. Finish the citations and finalize the internal links, being sure nothing is referred to by page number, since handhelds create their own page numbers.

Kindle™. 6 PM. Email the final draft to Joshua for Kindle™ formatting.

17-Jan-2010

I am typing this in advance, now, since the book will already be formatted at this point and additional content would just slow things down.

Rest. I will rest this day while Joshua works (he told me he rests on Saturdays).

Final Review. 5 PM. Joshua will send me the Kindle® rough draft for final review.

Last Outsourcing Step. Before bed, I will email Joshua any required changes.

18-Jan-2010

Mark's Birthday: Happy 23rd Birthday, Son!

Today Joshua will make the final changes and then help me upload the Kindle™-format to Amazon.com. It will take up to two weeks to be posted on their website, but as of today, it will be there.

I will finalize the handout notes for the library training and forward those to my contact who will email them to each library for pre-printing.

19-Jan-2010

Begin checking Amazon daily to know when to send the experts their free copy of the eBook along with an invitation to provide feedback at Amazon.com.

20-Jan-2010

12 Noon. The Pinch Hit Presentations begin. Thanks for thinking of me, Barb!

2-Feb-2010

Post Log. 8:39 AM. The eBook showed up on Amazon within 24 hours of submission. The positive feedback began trickling in immediately. The training sessions were going great, until the final day was rescheduled due to bad weather. On the day I was to be giving that final training, I embraced the possibility of POD (print on demand) and began pursuing that option. In 21 minutes, I have my conference with Gaines from CreateSpace to finalize the process that will take *eBooks* from electronic to paperback, prior to the rescheduled training event this Saturday. What a ride!

End Notes

(1) Cole, J. B., & Joffrey, R. (2005). *This Day in the Life Diaries from Women Across America*. New York: Three Rivers Press.

(2) Waller, J & Denning, T. (2009). The Blessing. On *The Blessing* [CD]. Genevoxl.

Appendix II

Write to Sell

Kathleen Krull is one of my all-time favorite authors. Not only is she an excellent writer with dozens of books to her credit, but she is an experienced editor who has written a useful handbook which helps writers and editors focus their work.

12 Keys to Writing Books That Sell is currently out of print; but there are still some copies floating around libraries and used bookstore sites. If you ever find one, buy it!

Included below are just a few of the dozens of questions editors must ask. Start by simply reading through the following list. Next, siphon your entire project through the net, and finally, conduct a chapter by chapter analysis.

Tenacious determination now could attract the attention of agents, editors and publishing companies later, while helping you succeed with the toughest critics of all: your average reader.

Editorial (Ed) Questions

1. Is this a good book, or does it have that potential?
   - Is it polished and previously edited?
   - Is it polished and previously edited?
   - Have you weeded out clichés and sentences that make no sense?

- Are you communicating with a reader, or are you merely indulging yourself?
- Is your style literate, clear, contemporary, and energetic?

2. Does the book come alive?
   - Does it make Ed laugh or cry or want to learn something new?
   - Does it make Ed want to skip lunch, dinner, or sex to finish reading it?
   - Is the title catchy and appealing?
   - Is it original?

3. Does the book have a clearly defined focus?
   - What are you promising to do? Can it be summed up in one sentence?
   - If your book is fiction, can you tell a story that keeps up the tension?
   - If you have a nonfiction book, does it contain a pervasive thread of argument?
   - Have you let the thesis overwhelm your material, making it preachy or didactic? Are you distracted by a "message," ignoring character or plot?
   - Does the focus jump around? Do you start off by concentrating on one theme or subject, and then go off on tangents, perhaps never getting back to your original premise?
   - Does each chapter part contribute to the whole?
   - Do you keep your destination in view?

4. Does the book have a clearly defined audience?
   - If your book is fiction, can you tell a story that keeps up the tension?
   - What sex, what age level, what interest group, what literacy rate?
   - Is it a bookstore book or an institutional (school and library) book? Or does it fall between the cracks?
   - Will it appeal to people who typically buy books?
   - Is the audience you're writing for large enough to justify the expense and energy of publishing your book?

5. Is the book original and fresh?
   - Have you contributed something fresh to the field you've chosen?
   - Is your topic enlivened with a sense of humor or wit?
   - If your book seems timely or topical now, will it still seem so a year down the road?
   - If your book capitalizes on current or upcoming events, does Ed have the capacity to publish it in time?
   - What is your competition and have you demonstrated that you know how your book differs from the competition? Is your book superior?

6. Does the book have integrity?
   - Are your facts error-free and consistent, your quotations accurate?
   - Is your research up-to-date? Can it be independently verified—are your steps logical enough for Ed or a freelance expert to trace?

- Have you plagiarized anyone else's ideas or material? Have you borrowed song lyrics or extensive text quotations without indicating the need to obtain permission from the copyright owner?

- Do you invade anyone's privacy, disclosing distorted or embarrassing information—or just plain information the person doesn't want disclosed?

- If you're writing fiction, do you use real names of people who are likely to become upset and even threaten a lawsuit?

- Do you substantiate assertions, especially controversial ones? Do you corroborate your information with reliable sources?

- Do you keep records of interview and research in case any of your facts are questioned later?

7. How much editorial work will the book require?

- Does what you've done need a lot of revision? What exactly are the weaknesses, and are they major (structural) or minor (easily fixed)?

- How much writing experience do you have? Are you the right person to complete the necessary revisions, or to do the book at all?

- Is your attitude pleasant? Are you easy to work with, professional, dedicated, or do you make unreasonable claims and demands? Are you serious about your work and willing to be guided toward making it better?

Marketing Questions

8. What are your credentials for writing this book?

- Does your experience demonstrate a passion for your topic and for writing? To what lengths have you gone to get your material and research?

- Are you intelligent and cooperative—a professional? Do you have integrity?

- Are you personable—enthusiastic, articulate, excited? Can you convey all this on paper until such time as you meet with Ed?

- Will you be a "team player" with the sales staff, or will you be off in a corner playing your own game?

9. Will the book make money?

- Does your book meet a need in the marketplace? Is it strong enough to compete in a crowded library market and crowded bookstores?

- What is the marketing staff's estimate of your first year's sales? Will the initial print run be high enough to justify production costs and impress key book sellers?

- Does your book have limited appeal (New Yorkers, say, or another regional audience), or a national, even universal appeal? How will it sell in Iowa (a state that has the highest rate per capita of books checked out of the library)?

Design & Production Questions

10. Can the book be produced economically, in a visually attractive package?

- Can an appropriate and economical cover be designed? Is there a scene, theme, character, or conflict that jumps out as good cover material?

- Does the project demand the complicated, the impossible, or the very expensive, in terms of illustration, photos, or layout?

- Will your book fit easily into an economical size and format that the publisher is accustomed to succeeding with? Are any aesthetic compromises necessary to produce the book economically? Would these harm sales?

- Are there technical difficulties or unusual expenses involved—photo research, permissions feeds, maps, charts, graphs, unusual trim size, full-color illustrations, paper engineering, special film work?

- What is the estimated unit cost of the book, and will this allow the book to be published at a price the market will bear? Does it leave any room for profit?

Subsidiary Rights Questions

11. Is the book suitable for films, translation, book clubs, the moon?

    - Does Ed believe in the book strongly enough to submit it to the rigorous review of the major or numerous smaller book clubs?

    - Will the book be able to cross the ocean to Great Britain and Europe? Does it have universal appeal, or is it strictly an American book?

    - Is it suitable for TV or films?

    - Will magazines or newspapers want to excerpt your work? Either before its publication (first serial rights) or afterward (second serial rights)?

    - Are parts of your book likely to be anthologized, for which permissions fees can be charged? Would any part of your book work as a textbook or an educational filmstrip?

12. Will the book survive on the backlist?
    - Is your book likely to be on best seller lists?
    - Is this a book that's groundbreaking or revolutionary in some way?
    - Do you have a potentially award-winning book?
    - Is your book of the type that could get "canonized"—entering the literary canon that's taught or anthologized in college or high school courses year after year? Are you one of the living writers being deemed "classic" by the literary establishment, women's and minority studies groups, nature writers, special interest groups in your field?
    - Will you have sequels or can you make a series out of it?

Adapted by permission from Krull, Kathleen. *12 Keys to Writing Books That Sell*. Cincinnati, Ohio: Writer's Digest, 1989. Visit www.kathleenkrull.com for more information.

Appendix III

Find a Writing Coach

Here are a handful of options, shown in alphabetical order.

Carol Adler, Write to Publish for Profit
http://www.write-to-publish-for-profit.com

Dr. Keith Barton, Virtual Writing Coach
http://www.virtualwritingcoach.com/newsletters/06november.htm

Angela Booth
http://iwritecoach.com/

Lou Bortone, The Book Writing Coach
http://www.theBookwritingcoach.com

Earma Brown
http://www.EarmaBrown.org

Keith Carol, Author Coaching
http://www.authorcoaching.com/

Joan Clout-Kruse, Write My Biz Book
http://www.powerhousewriting.com

Tiffany Colter, Writing Career Coach
http://writingcareercoach.com/

Melinda Copp
http://www.melindacopp.com

Judy Cullins, Book Coach

http://www.bookcoaching.com

Diane Eble, Words to Profit
http://www.wordstoprofit.com

Eddie Jones, Writer's Coach
http://www.writerscoach.us/

Allen R. Kates, Writing & Publishing
http://www.writingpublishing.com

Suzanne Lieurance, The Working Writer's Coach
http://www.workingwriterscoach.com

Bobbi Linkemer, The Invisible Presence Behind Your Nonfiction Book
http://www.writingandmarketingsecrets.com

Jacqui Lofthouse, The Writing Coach
http://www.thewritingcoach.co/uk/literary-consultancy.php

Sarah Lovett, Coach Sarah
http://www.writingcoachsarah.com/

Maria Mar, Writing is the Road to Your Dream
http://www.writetodream.com

Suzan St. Maur, Welcome Words
http://www.suzanstmaur.com

Bruce McAllister
http://www.mcallistercoaching.com/bio.html

Candace Sinclair, The Writers Mentor
http://www.thewritersmentor.com

Lisa Tener, Writing Coach

http://www.lisatener.com

Ellen Violette, The E-Book Coach
http://www.theeBookcoach.com

Jurgen Wolff, Your Writing Coach
http://www.yourwritingcoach.com

Joanna Young, Confident Writing
http://www.confidentwriting.com

Appendix IV

Research Like a Pro

Conducting research is one of my favorite things to do, when I have time. For this project, I needed to focus on team coordination and use my time writing the content of the chapters.

As I model in Appendix XV, I hired several outsourcers to conduct my research. I retained Vijay Marathe as my research coordinator for future projects. His skills are exceptional and working with him a joy. His main interest lies in web research and copy writing. However, he is also skilled in Search Engine Optimization (SEO).

The following tips are a gift to you, from Vijay, for times when you want to be your own research guru.

1. To find blogs on your topic, the Google search engine http://blogsearch.google.com is the best option. Another good option is http://news.search.yahoo.com.

2. There are a few operators that can help in getting filtered search results, but the Google robot is smart enough to find exactly what you are looking for. It is best to stick to very simple research query requests.

3. http://www.google.com/intl/en/help/operators.html can be helpful at times.

4. Using a very concise phrase for the topic searching is the key to help Google give you the most relevant listings.

5. Use your ingenuity to figure out words and phrases that are most likely to appear on your ideal page. For example, while searching for blogs that provide information for non-fiction and 'how-to' authorship, I used phrases such as: *tips, non-fiction, authors, writers, guide to self-publishing, diy (do it yourself) writers authors, resources self-publishing, POD (print on demand) authors,* and so on. It is best to visualize from the blog writer's point of view while brainstorming for effective search queries.

6. The most important part is to quickly scan through the blog post to differentiate between the good blogs and the not-so good ones. Look for typos: if the writer is not interested in taking efforts at editing, you can rest assured he/she is only interested in getting his/her page indexed with the help of a lot of questionable links and copied content. Good blogs always convey a sense of altruism and the writers readily recommend other good writers even for the same topic.

Note from Marnie: Just as a skilled researcher, like Vijay, rates the quality of a blog based on grammar and typos, so our readers rank our professionalism based on our book's editing. Remember: edit, edit, edit!

Vijay is an ODesk outsourcer whose private profile is visible to members only.

Appendix V

Meet the eBook Architect

Joshua Tallent, the eBook Architect, started http://www.KindleFormatting.com right after the Amazon Kindle was first released. He has formatted a large number of books for a diverse set of individual authors and small publishers, and has had the opportunity to work with books from a broad range of subject categories. He was the Kindle and Smashwords formatter for the eBook versions of this book, and I highly recommend him to you.

Joshua Writes

As the eBook Architect, I provide consultation services to a variety of clients, from big companies like LibreDigital and Rand McNally, to small presses and independent authors. I enjoy answering eBook-related questions.

The number one question I get is: "If I can just upload my Word document or PDF to the Kindle store, why would I need to hire you?"

As the following Q&As show, the transformation process a book goes through from hardcopy to electronic text is always a challenge; every book is different, and every project brings unique obstacles and issues.

I love my work... there's never a dull moment! And, as anyone who knows me can tell you, I am a stickler for quality and precision. Of course, you can do it yourself, and the following tips will help, but if you hit a bump or just want it done fast and to the highest standards possible, give me a call.

Questions & Answers

Q. I uploaded my PDF to the DTP but it looks horrible. What happened to my formatting?

A. Unfortunately, the DTP does not support PDF uploads as well as it does other formats. Actually, Amazon suggests that you upload an HTML file, since the Kindle/Mobipocket format is based on HTML. PDF files are made specifically for print media and are not really designed to work with eBook readers.

Q. Why can't I dictate what shows up on each page of my book on the Kindle?

A. The Kindle format is based on HTML, which allows the user much more control as they read the book. For instance, the user can change the font size in the book on-the-fly, and the text will flow differently on the page as a result. This means that "pages" (in the common hardcopy book sense) are not present on the Kindle. eBooks in general take a much more flexible approach to pagination. This is also why the Kindle has a "Location" indicator at the bottom of the screen. That feature allows the reader to see their relative position in the book.

Q. You mean that there are no page numbers on the Kindle?

A. Precisely. Page numbers become mostly irrelevant on the Kindle and in other eBooks. For the most part, the only times they are useful are when the eBook contains references to other places in the text (these references should all be linked) or when there is an index at the end of the book (which should also be linked).

Q. So, my subject Index can be preserved in my eBook?

A. Yes! It is not hard to make an index work in an eBook, you just have to insert "page number" anchors in the text and point the index to those anchors.

Q. Okay, PDFs are not preferred, but what format should I use for uploading my book?

A. Well, as I mentioned before, HTML is the format preferred by Amazon, but you can do a decent job of formatting the book yourself in Microsoft Word. The key to using Word is to utilize the built-in Styles mechanism so that your book is consistent and well-formed. Of course, this can become a pretty formidable job, especially for someone who is in a hurry or someone without the skills, tools, or patience for such a task. That is when you can contact me.

Q. I have tried sending my book to my Kindle, but the images are never included. Can I preview my book on the Kindle without having to upload it to the DTP and buy a copy?

A. Yes, you can easily Preview your book on your own Kindle with the images intact.

This process will require that you download and install Mobipocket Creator, but don't be intimidated by that.

    1. Open Mobipocket Creator.

    2. Select "HTML Document" from the section "Import from an Existing File".

    3. Browse to the HTML file and press "Import".

    4. This will generate a folder in your My Documents\My Publications folder that the same as your HTML file.

5. Open that folder and copy into it any images that are in your book.

6. In Creator, select "Build" from the Menu.

7. On the Build page, press the "Build" button.

8. Go back to your book folder. You will now see a .opf file and a .prc file.

9. Plug in your Kindle and copy the .prc file to your "documents"folder, or e-mail the file to your Kindle.com address.

Q. Why do you charge so much?

A. Well, I honestly think my services are worth the cost. Most books only require a few hours of work, so the total cost of the conversion to Kindle's format is usually around $200. That is a small price to pay for a book that looks good and will be easy on your readers' eyes. If you find yourself unable to come up with that type of investment, drop me a line and we can talk about options. Sometimes just one hour spent working on a book can make a big difference for my clients. I am usually able to finish more in that one hour than an author unfamiliar with HTML can do in a few days.

Q. Will my eBook look like my hardcopy?

A. Yes and no. There are some elements of a hardcopy that can be retained in an eBook. However, there are some limitations to the amount of formatting that can be forced into the Kindle mold. I have been able to do some very difficult formatting for my clients, but if your book has specific formatting, you should be prepared to see it tweaked in the eBook.

Q. What do you need to get started?

A. If you have an original Word document that is almost always the best file to work from. If you have a PDF, that will work as well. Historically PDF files take longer to process than Word documents since the code behind the scenes is usually much messier and more bloated.

Q. What if I don't have an electronic file?

A. It is possible to scan and convert your hardcopy book into an electronic file, and from that into a Kindle book. This process will take longer and will include some extra charges associated with the scanning, but it is a great option for getting an out-of-print book into the Kindle format, and even opens up the possibility of making the book available in print form again.

Note: Joshua joined me live during the PRO Author Training. The download of our interview is available from http://www.LeadershipAttitudes.com. Be sure to visit Joshua's website: http://www.ebookarchitect.com.

Appendix VI

Format for Handheld Readers & POD

Unless you have a big budget, or friends eager to provide technical support, your goal is to prepare a manuscript that can be easily converted to a PDF for handheld and POD formatting.

When I began writing eBooks in the late 90's, I purchased Adobe's PDF Writer. The cost of that program today is $299. Since then many other options have been developed. The following are free PDF creation tools. Each tool has its own set of instructions:

DocuDesk
http://www.docudesk.com/deskPDF_PDF_Creator_select_your_version_2.shtml?utm_nooverride=1&gclid=COrjlaHGyZ8CFRHxDAodGzFl3g

gDoc™ Products
http://www.globalgraphics.com/en/gdoc

PrimoPDF
http://www.primopdf.com/index.aspx

Blogger, Charles Pooter, put together a comparison chart including many other options. It was written before the release of gDoc, so that one is not reviewed. You may read his article here:
http://www.littlemanwhatnow.com/2006/07/review-of-free-pdf-creation-software.html

Formatting & Uploading Providers

The following are US freelancers, but remember that both ODesk and Elance feature outsource providers as well.

You will want to find someone skilled in formatting and uploading eBooks and PODs to any of the major sites. For eBooks, inquire about their experience uploading to Amazon's Kindle™ Store, Smashwords, Scribd, Shortcovers, Lulu and eBookMall and ask about their success formatting in all of the most popular formats, including ePub, Mobi Pocket, eReader, LIT, Smashwords and PDF.

This eBook was formatted and uploaded by
EBook Architect, Joshua Tallent
http://www.eBookarchitects.com

Here is a list of other service providers:

Nom de Plume
http://www.eBookformatting.com/

Wordclay
http://www.wordclay.com/ServicesStore/ServicesStoreServiceDetails.aspx?ImprintServiceID=1027

EBook Conversion Services
http://eBookconversion.com/

Lulu
http://www.lulu.com/product/service/amazon-Kindle-eBook-formatting-service/4982891

Zacton Press
http://www.zactonpress.com/eBook_format.html

Virtual Gal Friday:
http://www.virtualgalfriday.com/virtual_assistant_services/eBook-formatting-design.html

Mostcool Media, Inc.
http://www.mostcoolmedia.com/eBook_editing.htm

EBook Graphics
http://www.eBookgraphics.com/index.html

The Virtual Peach
http://thevirtualpeach.com/services/eBook-formatting-and-editing-services

Appendix VII

Create a Cool Cover

Malcolm Gladwell hit another homerun with his book, *Outliers* (1). When I looked just now, it was ranked #13 in Amazon and had 834 reviews with an average 4-star ranking. Impressive!

But have you seen the cover? It features two things: Malcolm Gladwell's name and the title.

Here's my advice: unless your name is Malcolm, or this is your umpteenth best seller, you might not want to try that.

Your Graphics Have Got to Grab Attention

Design Guru, Ryan T. Jackson, explains,

> "The e-book cover design must look amazingly tangible so that the visitor wants to reach in and grab it. The only way a cover graphic will sell your service or product, is by matching your content. If you opt for a professionally designed cover, with clarity, polish, impact and sharpness, then you will increase your sales, purely based on presentation. After all, how do most salesmen dress?" (2)

Angela Booth, author of *Sell Your Writing Online* NOW says,

> "A great eBook with quality information will keep selling for you for years. Good graphics and bonuses

will increase your sales every day, with just a little extra effort." (3)

Graphic Artists for Hire

The cover of this book was designed by Erin Adler, Lauren Graphics, Inc. http://www.laurengraphicsinc.com

Additional Options

1106
http://1106design.com/

Cherished Solutions
http://www.cherishedsolutions.com/cs/

Corvus Design Studio & Publishing Services
http://www.corvusdesignstudio.com/

Creative EBook Design
http://www.creativeeBookdesign.com/

F+P Graphic Design, Inc.
http://fpgd.com/

Daniel Holeman
http://www.awakenvisions.com/GraphicDesign.html

Karen Saunders, MacGraphics
http://www.macgraphics.net/

Michele Renée Ledoux
http://www.cipabooks.com/associates/graphic_artists.htm

Purple Fish Media
http://www.purplefishmedia.com/

Cathi Stevenson
http://www.bookcoverexpress.com/

Joyce Mihran Turley
http://www.dixoncovedesign.com/newprojects.html

End Notes

(1) Gladwell, Malcolm. (2008). *Outliers: The Story of Success*. New York, Ny: Little, Brown and Company; 1 edition (November 18, 2008)

(2) Top 5 Myths About Learning To Play Piano at Sell Used... (n.d.). Retrieved from http://www.sellusedmicrophones.com/?keywords=Top+5+Myths+About+Learning+To+Play+Piano

(3) "EBooks - Graphics and Bonuses Help You to Sell" Top EBook Writer. (n.d.). Retrieved from http://www.topeBookwriter.com/strategies/eBooks-graphics-and-bonuses-help-you-to-sell-51/

Appendix VIII

Get Your ISBN

Obtaining an International Standard Book Number (ISBN) used to take weeks. Imagine my delight when I received my ISBN less than fifteen minutes after starting the online ordering process. Note: This was my experience and is no guarantee that your ISBN will be available that quickly.

At the time of this writing, a single ISBN costs $125 while buying them in sets provides notable savings.

An ISBN number is required before uploading any eBook to Amazon's Kindle™ Store.

Prior to requesting yours, be sure you can answer these questions:

1. Will your copyright be under your own name or that of a business?
2. Will you be registering for foreign or domestic rights or both?
3. Who will you assign as your ISBN coordinator/contact person?
4. What online payment method will you use to pay for your ISBN? (2010: $125)
5. Will you need priority processing? (Extra $75)
6. Do you need the physical bar code (to photocopy and apply on a paper copy), or is the ISBN number itself sufficient? There is an extra fee for the physical bar*.

7. Distribution Information: where will your books be sold?

*Here is a hint I happened upon while doing my research. I had registered for a free account with LuLu.com to check out their process. On one of the first screens, it invites you to enter your own ISBN so it can generate the barcode. At this stage, you have not paid for any services yet. So, basically, as of this writing, this is one free way for you to obtain your barcode.

When you are ready to apply for your ISBN:

1. Go to http://www.MyIdentifiers.com.
2. Select: "ISBN Number" and "Buy Now."
3. Create an account.
4. Enter the required information.
5. Submit payment.
6. Watch your email for your new ISBN number.

CreateSpace and Lulu (and probably others) offer free ISBN numbers when you engage their POD services. There is a lengthy article about the pros and cons of these offers here: http://www.publetariat.com/publish/truth-about-createspaces-free-isbns.

Note from my rep at Amazon.com: You are able to upload corrections to your original content, using the same ISBN number, unless your changes exceed 10% of the entire content, at which point you should order a new ISBN and publish it as a separate volume.

It is important to know that your feedback record is attached to your ISBN. You may post a new version under that same ISBN and retain your feedback results; but if you publish a new edition, your feedback record begins from scratch under that new ISBN.

Appendix IX

Sell Your eBook

As I mentioned earlier, my eBooks have been selling on my own websites for years. In fact, that is how most eBooks have sold until just recently. Many authors gain a steady stream of income by selling their resources independently.

The advent of handheld readers has opened many new options for eBook authors and buyers, some of which may increase your sphere of influence.

There are two site categories below. The first list provides the opportunity for authors to upload their eBooks for sale, while the second allows uploads for give-away.

As with all other website links and options included in this book, we have no control over the link functionality or the availability of the offer at any date later than today. We apologize, in advance, that at least a few of these links or services will no longer be available to you at some point. The information is included to inform you of some of the options available to you, to the best of our ability.

Partial List of Sites Allowing Authors to Upload Their Books To Be Sold

Amazon

http://www.Amazon.com

Barnes & Noble
http://www.barnesandnoble.com

Books on Board
http://www.booksonboard.com

Borders
http://www.borders.com

Café Book Shop
http://www.cafebookshop.com

Dragon Club
http://www.dragonclub.com

eBooks.com
http://www.ebooks.com

eBookstore
http://www.cambridge.org/ebookstore

eHarlequin eBook Store
http://www.ebooks.eharlequin.com

Mobipocket
http://www.mobipocket.com

O'Reilly Media
http://oreilly.com/store

Powell's Books
http://www.powells.com/ebookstore/ebooks.html

Random House, Inc.
http://www.randomhouse.com/category/ebooks/

Reader Store
http://ebookstore.sony.com

Todo eBook
http://www.todoebook.com

Partial List of Sites Allowing Authors to Upload Their Books To Be Given Away Free

Bookyards
http://www.bookyards.com

Dleex
http://www.dleex.com

Free Book Spot
http://www.freebookspot.com

Free eBooks and Software
http://www.snipfiles.com

Get Free eBooks
http://www.getfreeebooks.com

Globusz Publishing
http://www.globusz.com

KnowFree.net
http://knowfree.net

Many Books
http://manybooks.net

Online Computer Books
http://www.onlinecomputerbooks.com

Online Free eBooks
http://www.onlinefreeebooks.net

Zillr
http://www.zillr.org

Appendix X
Engage Your Local Library

Press Release: eBook and Audiobook Download Websites for Libraries See Record Growth in 2009. Used by permission.

OverDrive Library Partners Lend More Than 8.7 Million Digital Titles Including Most Downloaded Book "The Lost Symbol" by Dan Brown. (Boston, MA) - January 13, 2010

OverDrive (www.overdrive.com), the global leader in eBook and audiobook distribution, today announced significant milestones in library download circulation and web traffic in 2009. Patrons at more than 10,000 OverDrive-powered libraries worldwide viewed 401 million download website pages and checked out 8.7 million eBook, audiobook, music and video titles, both of which are all-time highs. On the heels of this record-breaking year for library downloads, OverDrive will demonstrate its success in enabling access to more than 300,000 eBook, audiobook, music, and video titles on popular devices, including PC, Mac®, iPod®, iPhone®, Zune®, Windows Mobile®, Sony® ReaderTM, nookTM, and DROIDTM by Motorola®, at ALA Midwinter in Boston (booth #2446), January 15-18, 2010.

In 2009, OverDrive partners achieved this substantial increase in usage as a result of the growing popularity of eBooks, iPod-compatibility for nearly all audiobooks in its catalog, and new mobile initiatives for wireless downloading, among other enhancements. Key statistics and milestones for OverDrive-powered libraries include:

-- 401 million website pages viewed by library patrons (69 percent growth over 2008) and 8.7 million digital titles checked out (63 percent increase over 2008)
-- 4 billion minutes of spoken word audio downloaded from library websites
-- 70 percent increase in audiobook checkouts over 2008, while eBook checkouts increased by 53 percent
-- 40 percent increase in new library users over 2008

-- The OverDrive digital catalog for libraries grew to 300,000 titles with the addition of 100,000 eBooks, 27,000 audiobooks, and 4,000 music and video titles
-- Using new Facebook® and TwitterTM sharing features, library users shared what they were downloading from their library thousands of times
-- OverDrive launched mobile versions of nearly all library download websites and released audiobook apps for Windows Mobile and Android phones

Dan Brown's international blockbuster "The Lost Symbol" was the most downloaded adult fiction audiobook and eBook of 2009 from the library. Titles from Stephenie Meyer, Malcolm Gladwell, and Barack Obama were also among the most downloaded books from the library in 2009. Top five titles in each adult category include:

Most Downloaded Adult Fiction Audiobooks from the Library (2009)
(Title, Author, Publisher)
1. "The Lost Symbol," Dan Brown, Books on Tape
2. "The Host," Stephenie Meyer, Books on Tape
3. "The Associate," John Grisham, Books on Tape
4. "Atlas Shrugged," Ayn Rand, Blackstone Audio, Inc.
5. "The 8th Confession," James Patterson, Books on Tape

Most Downloaded Adult Fiction eBooks from the Library (2009)
(Title, Author, Publisher)

1. "The Lost Symbol," Dan Brown, Knopf Doubleday Publishing Group
2. "Devil in Winter," Lisa Kleypas, HarperCollins
3. "Again the Magic," Lisa Kleypas, HarperCollins
4. "Because You're Mine," Lisa Kleypas, HarperCollins
5. "Dreaming of You," Lisa Kleypas, HarperCollins

Most Downloaded Adult Nonfiction Audiobooks from the Library (2009)
(Title, Author, Publisher)

1. "25 Things to Say to the Interviewer to Get the Job You Want," Dexter
   Hawk, Blackstone Audio
2. "Outliers," Malcolm Gladwell, Books on Tape
3. "Blink," Malcolm Gladwell, Books on Tape
4. "Three Cups of Tea," Greg Mortenson, Tantor Media
5. "The 4-Hour Work Week," Timothy Ferriss, Blackstone Audio

Most Downloaded Adult Nonfiction eBooks from the Library (2009)
(Title, Author, Publisher)

1. "Blink," Malcolm Gladwell, Little, Brown and Company
2. "The 100 Simple Secrets of Successful People," David Niven,
   HarperCollins
3. "Marley & Me," John Grogan, HarperCollins
4. "Dreams from My Father," Barack Obama, Crown Publishing Group
5. "Change Your Brain, Change Your Life," Daniel G. Amen, M.D., Crown
   Publishing Group

OverDrive also releases monthly 'Most Downloaded Books from the Library' lists, which showcase the most popular digital book titles at OverDrive-powered public libraries. To see what library users are downloading each month, visit http://overdrive.com/mostdownloaded.

OverDrive also operates the Digital Bookmobile (www.digitalbookmobile.com), a high-tech 18-wheeler traveling North America on behalf of public libraries to raise awareness about free library downloads. In 2009, the Digital Bookmobile held 155 events with public libraries in 34 states and provinces. Since the tour launched in August of 2008, the Digital Bookmobile has traveled more than 25,000 miles and trained more than 35,000 library users on download services from their library.

To see if your public library is a member of the OverDrive network, visit http://search.overdrive.com.

About OverDrive
OverDrive is a leading full-service digital distributor of eBooks, audiobooks, music, and video. We deliver secure management, DRM protection, and download fulfillment services for hundreds of publishers and thousands of libraries, schools, and retailers, serving millions of end users. OverDrive has been named to the EContent 100 as a company that matters most in the digital content industry. Founded in 1986, OverDrive is based in Cleveland, OH.
www.overdrive.com

Media Contact:
David Burleigh
Director of Marketing
OverDrive, Inc.
dburleigh@overdrive.com

216-573-6886 Ext 218

Note: David Burleigh is a featured guest at the PRO Author Training available from http://www.LeadershipAttitudes.com.

During that interview, he mentioned the list of 1000+ partner publishers available at this website URL: http://www.contentreserve.com/pubpartner.asp.

If you opt to research publishers for your book, be sure their names are on this list before making your final choice. Libraries account for thousands of book sales per year.

Appendix XI
Progress Toward Paperback Publication

Friday, January 29, 2010. 5:01 PM

Deep breathing to relax. I cannot believe that I have made this project so complex. It would give even the bravest warrior nightmares.

Yowsa! What was I thinking?!

I suppose my greatest huffing and puffing at the moment stems from the reality that I have only a handful of days until my two major publicity launches, the blog blast and PRO Author Training, and I have yet to finalize the manuscript or determine a clear winner for who will publish my paperback.

This paperback publication step feels terrifyingly permanent compared to the fluidity of an eBook.

Tuesday, February 02, 2010. 9:12 AM

Speaking with Gaines from CreateSpace, I ask, "How hard is it to request a reprint if I find a mistake in my book after it goes to print?"

Answer: "Easy! You re-submit it, wait for the preview copy, pay for it, approve it, and the new version is published. It's that simple."

As of right now, paperback printing is no longer final nor irrevocable. It is as fluid as an eBook and that makes this doable for every PRO Author.

I take a deep breath, lift up a prayer and keep going: I keep putting one foot in front of the other, taking the steps that seem feasible at the moment.

I Love LuLu

I am not publishing with LuLu, but I've got to admit that it is the nicest, most user-friendly option I've found.

Just now, for example, I am using the template from Lulu.com to format my book for upload to CreateSpace. Earlier, I used the ISBN bar code generator to render the image I needed for my back jacket.

Someday, I am going to find a way to pay LuLu back for providing these services at no cost and with no obligation. I am impressed!

A Few Great Articles Comparing POD Services

An entire book could be written comparing your Print on Demand publishing options. Suffice it to say that I finally chose both CreateSpace and Lightning Source. You will have to decide for yourself.

The following are some of the articles that do a really good job explaining your options. I encourage you, in addition, to speak with a sales rep at the companies you are considering. I learned so much during my short conversations with Gaines at CreateSpace and Dorothy at LightningSource.

Do not be afraid to ask your questions. This is an important decision.

Story Hack, Bryce Beattie

Choosing a "free" POD publisher: Lulu vs Createspace

http://www.storyhack.com/2008/12/06/choosing-a-free-pod-publisher-lulu-vs-createspace/

Indie Author, April Hamilton

Lulu vs. CreateSpace: Which Is More Economical for the DIY Author?

http://aprillhamilton.blogspot.com/2009/03/lulu-vs-createspace-which-is-more.html

Yen Relish

POD Publisher Comparison
http://www.yenrelish.com/2009/11/pod-publisher-comparison.html

Still Alive, Nitsa

What Print on Demand Should You Use?
http://nonphotography.com/blog/?p=570

Professional Personal Historian, Dan Curtis

5 Print-On-Demand Sites You'll Want to Consider

http://dancurtis.ca/2010/01/06/5-print-on-demand-sites-youll-want-to-consider/

The LL Book Review, Shannon Yarbrough

How Does Lightning Source Compare to Lulu and Createspace?

http://llbookreview.com/2009/06/how-does-lightning-source-compare-to-lulu-and-createspace/

Appendix XII

Choose a Paperback Publisher

As you have probably deduced by now, I am an extreme DIY: Do It Yourselfer.

If you prefer to have help, there are dozens of options for you. Again, this is not an easy decision. But, as you go through the list and visit the sites, you will find yourself drawn to some more than others. Take notes.

Contact the representative from those that intrigue, and narrow down your options to a handful of finalists. Next, do a comparison of the pros and cons before making your decision.

Note: There are probably many publishers we have missed. The * (asterisk) next to a publishing company indicates its inclusion at the Lightning Source website.

1st World Publishing*
http://www.1stworldpublishing.com
Leah Waller
leah@1stworldpublishing.com
877-209-5004

48-Hour Books
http://www.48hrbooks.com
info@48hrbooks.com
800-231-0521

360 Digital Books
http://www.360inc.com
Kim Warner, Sales Account Manager
kwarner@360inc.com
866-379-8767
Fax: 734-591-7899

A&A Printing
http://www.printshopcentral.com
Billy Ashby
billy@printshopcentral.com
866-886-0065

Advantage Media Group
http://www.advantageww.com
Ben Toy
btoy@advantageww.com
800-848-3180

Alexander's Print Advantage
http://www.alexanders.com
Gwen Gades
gweng@alexanders.com
800-574-8666

America's Press
http://www.americas-press.com
Joel Turner
joelt@americas-press.com (East Coast)
Victor Judd
victorj@americas-press.com (West Coast)
281-557-4300

Ames On-Demand
http://www.amesondemand.com
Jose Colon
jcolon@amesondemand.com
617-684-1132

Angel Printing
http://www.angelprint.com
Vladimir Medvinsky
books@angelprint.com
760-967-0492

Apex Book Manufacturing
http://www.apexbm.com
Almad Meradji
ahmad@apexbm.com
877-TEL-APEX

Area Printing & Design
http://www.areaprinting.com

Neal Sumlin
csumlin@areaprinting.com
877-268-9110

Author House
http://www.authorhouse.com
Tom Britt
tbritt@authorhouse.com
800-839-8640
Fax: 812-339-6554

Automated Graphic Systems
http://www.ags.com
Adam Rutkowski
info@ags.com
800-678-8760

AuthorSolutions*
http://www.authorsolutions.com
Form: http://www.authorsolutions.com/ContactUs.aspx?ekfrm=32

Aventine Press*
http://www.aventinepress.com
Brion Sausser, Managing Editor
editor@aventinepress.com
866-246-6142

Black Forest Press*
http://www.blackforestpress.net
authorinfo@blackforestpress.net
423-422-4711

Blurb.com
http://www.blurb.com
Eileen Gittins, CEO

BookBlocks
http://www.bookblocks.com
Kumar Persad
info@bookblocks.com
800-836-7581, ext. 111

Booklocker.com, Inc*
http://www.booklocker.com
Form: http://www.booklocker.com/help/contact.html

BookMobile.com
http://www.bookmobile.com
Nicole Baxter
nbaxter@bookmobile.com
800-752-3303
Fax: 612-677-3271

Book1One
http://www.book1one.com
George Kittredge

georgek@book1one.com
585-647-8919, ext. 216

Books Just Books
http://www.rjc-lcc.com
Ron Pramschufer
Ron@rjc-lcc.com
800-621-2556
Fax: 212-681-8002

Borders Personal Publishing (Lulu)
http://www.lulu.com

Business Graphics
http://www.bizreplication.com
Jeff Carter
jcarter@bizreplication.com
800-265-7269
Fax: 916-772-2332

Buy Books On The Web
http://www.buybooksontheweb.com
info@buybooksontheweb.com
877-BUY-BOOK
Fax: 610-941-9959

CafePress
http://www.cafepress.com
877-809-1659

Central Plains Book Manufacturing
http://www.centralplainsbook.com
Melody Morris
mmorris@centralplainsbook.com
877-278-2726
Fax: 316-221-4762

Colorwise Commercial Printing
http://www.colorwise.com
bestbook@colorwise.com
888-664-8166
Fax: 770-664-8145

Commercial Communications
http://www.comcom.com
info@comcom.com
800-DOCUTECH
Fax: 262-369-5647

Consolidated Reprographics
http://www.consrepro.com
Susanne D'Arcy
sdarcy@consrepro.com
714-966-2164

Stuart F. Cooper Printers
http://www.sfcooper.com
Joseph Silverman

joes@sfcooper.com
800-421-8703
Fax: 213-747-3035

Copresco
http://www.copresco.com
Steve Johnson
steve@copresco.com
630-690-2000

The Copy Center
http://www.thecopycenterplus.com
print@thecopycenterplus.com
207-623-1452

The Country Press
http://www.countrypressinc.com
Michael Pinto
info@countrypressinc.com
508-947-4485
Fax: 508-947-8989

Crane Duplicating Services
http://www.cranduplicating.com
Dick Price, President
dick@craneduplicating.com
508-958-4877
Fax: 508-760-1544

CreateSpace, Amazon's Site
http://www.createspace.com/
Gaines Hill, Publishing Consultant
877-814-3488 ext. 8137

Creative Imaging
http://www.creativeimaginginc.com
Bernie Bahn
bbahn@creativeimaginginc.com
636-717-0690
Fax: 636-717-0695

CSS Publishing / Fairway Press
http://www.csspub.com
David Runk
david@csspub.com
800-241-4056
Fax: 419-222-4647

DeHart's Printing Services Corporation
http://www.deharts.com
leads@deharts.com
888-982-4763

DiggyPod
http://www.diggypod.com
Tim Simpson
tim@diggypod.com
734-944-7844

Fax: 734-429-3309

Digital Impressions
http://www.digimpressions.com
Blair Meason Fredericksburg
blair@digimpressions.com
540-752-1011

Digital Marketing Technologies
http://www.dmtpublishing.com
Mark Manser
mark@dmtpublishing.com
801-397-1826

Documation LLC
http://www.documation.com
Roy Fuerstenberg, President
royf@documation.com
800-951-6729
Fax: 715-836-7411

Dog Ear Publishing*
http://www.dogearpublishing.net
Alan, Miles, or Ray
help-me@dogearpublishing.net
866-823-9613

Dreams Publishing
http://www.dreamspublishing.com

Teresa Rhodes, Acquisition Director
acquisitions@DreamsPublishing.com

eBookStand
http://www.bookstandpublishing.com
Marilyn Jenkins, President
authorservices@bookstandpublishing.com
425-315-1434
Fax: 425-315-8835

Edition One Books
http://www.editiononestudios.com
Ben Zlotkin
info@editiononestudios.com
510-705-1930

Elderberry Press, Inc*
http://www.elderberrypress.com
Mr. St. John
editor@elderberrypress.com
541-459-6043

Express Press
http://www.expresspress.com
David Clar
sales@expresspress.com
877-552-5047

Faulkner Strategies

http://www.faulknerstrategies.com
Kevin Walters
kevin@faulknerstrategies.com
574-272-4671
Fax: 574-272-4695

Fidlar Doubleday
http://www.fidlardoubleday.com
cusservice@fidlardoubleday.com
800-248-0888
Fax: 1 800 884 2437

FlexPress
http://www.flexpress.com
W P Ward, COO
sales@flexpress.com
972-980-2631, x218
Fax: 972-980-8136

Gom Publishing
http://www.gompublishing.com
communications@gompublishing.com
866-GOM-2608
Fax: 866-422-8292

Green Button
http://www.greenbuttoninc.com
Joanne Hoyt
joanneh@greenbuttoninc.com

570-674-2975

The Gregath Publishing Company
http://www.gregathcompany.com
book@gregathcompany.com
918-542-4148

Guild of Blades Retail Group
http://www.guildofblades.com
Ryan Johnson
dowrie@guildofblades.com
248-430-4980

Hill Print Solutions
http://www.hillprintsolutions.com
Mitchell Hill
mitchell@hillprintsolutions.com
214-826-0092

HubCast
http://www.hubcast.com
Sales@hubcast.com
877-207-6665

Infinity Publishing*
http://www.infinitypublishing.com
Form:
http://www.infinitypublishing.com/component/option,com_chronocontact/Itemid,167/

877-BUYBOOK
Fax: 610-941-9959

Infinity Publishing
http://www.buybooksontheweb.com
info@buybooksontheweb.com
610-941-9999
Fax: 610-941-9959

Inkwater Press
http://www.inkwaterpress.com
info@inkwaterpress.com
503-968-6777
Fax: 503-968-6779

InstaBook Corporation
http://www.instabook-corporation.com
Victor Celorio, President
ibc@instabook-corporation.com

InstantPublisher.com
http://www.instantpublisher.com
Chris Bradley
cbradleyip@gmail.com
800-259-2592

iUniverse*
http://www.iuniverse.com

Form:
http://www.iuniverse.com/ContactUs/ContactUs.aspx
800-AUTHORS
FAX: 812-355-4085

King Printing
http://www.kingprinting.com
Tom Campbell
tcampbell@kingprinting.com
978-458-2345
Fax: 978-458-3026

Lightning Press Printing Group*
http://www.ligntnight-press.com
sales@lightning-press.com
973-890-4422
Fax: 973-890-4414

Lightning Source*
http://www.lightningsource.com
inquiry@lightningsource.com
615-213-5815
Fax: 615-213-4425

Llumina Press*
http://www.llumina.com
Deborah Dawson
ddawson@llumina.com
866-229-9244

LuLu*
http://www.lulu.com
Stephen Fraser, Marketing Manager
sfraser@lulu.com

Mandeville Press
http://www.mandevillepress.org
books@mandevillepress.org
323-737-4055
Fax: 323-737-5680

Masthof Press
http://www.masthof.com
Dan Mast
dan@masthof.com
610-286-0258

Medius Corporation
http://www.mediuscorp.com
tony@mediuscorp.com
408-519-5000
Fax: 408-519-5001

Metropolis Ink
http://www.metropolisink.com
support@metropolisink.com
928-427-0329
Fax: 928-427-9488

Monument Press
http://www.monumentpress.net
Form: http://www.monumentpress.net/contact.html
901-328-7206

Morgan James Publishing, LLC*
http://www.ingrampublisherservices.com
customerservice@ingrampublisherservices.com
800-485-4943

NetPublications
http://www.netpub.net
William R. Grogg, President
custservice@netpub.net
800-724-1100
Fax: 845-463-0018

Nightengale Press*
http://www.nightengalepress.com
Valerie Connelly
vconnelly47@yahoo.com
847-810-8498
Fax: 866-830-2624

No Waste Publishing
http://www.nowastepublishing.com
bookhelp@nowastepublishing.com
866-845-BOOK

Lisa Fox extension 103

Offset Paperback Manufacturers
http://www.opm.com
Nancy Lavan
nancy.lavan@opm.com
570-675-5261
Fax: 570-674-9407

On Demand Machine Corporation
http://www.bookmachine.com
Harvey Ross, President
information@bookmachine.com
314-878-3695
Fax: 314-878-6429

On-Demand Technologies
http://www.on-demandtech.com
Merna Tontat
mtontat@on-demandtech.com
800-438-1826

Outskirts Press*
http://www.outskirtspress.com/authors.php
info@outskirtspress.com
1-888-OP-BOOKS

Paraview Books
http://www.cosimobooks.com

Form:
http://www.cosimobooks.com/cosimo/contact_us.html
212-989-3616

Philadelphia Print and Color
http://www.philadelphiaprint.com
Jeff Iegman
info@philadelphiaprint.com
215-563-2200
Fax: 215-563-3212

Picaboo.com
http://www.picaboo.com
Form: http://www.picaboo.com/support/contact.html

Plastic Card Factory
http://www.plasticcardfactory.com
info@PlasticCardFactory.com
866-539-7231
Fax: 561-202-9829

P.O.D. Wholesale
http://www.podwholesale.com
info@podwholesale.com
610-520-2500

Profits Publishing
http://www.profitspublishing.com
Marian Turgeon

marian@profitspublishing.com
Fax: 250-493-6603

Publish America*
http://www.publishamerica.com
Acquisitions@publishamerica.com

Publishers' Graphics
http://www.pubgraphics.com
Kathleen Marada
kathleen@pubgraphics.com
888-404-3769
Fax: 630-221-1870

Rapid Reproduction
http://www.raprepro.com
rapid@raprepro.com
978-657-6186
Fax: 978-988-7994

RPI Print
http://www.rpiprint.com
Ted Reischling, President
ted@rpiprint.com
206-371-0680

SelfPublishing.com*
http://www.selfpublishing.com
Form: http://www.selfpublishing.com/contact/

800-621-2556
Fax: 212-681-8002

SgtBlu Press
http://www.sgtblu.com
Form: http://sgtblu.com/contact
901-371-6525

Shared Ink
http://www.sharedink.com
support@sharedink.com
425-844-8920

Side Kick Printing
http://www.sidekickprinting.com
info@sidekickprinting.com
270-422-7944

Sir Speedy Atlanta
http://www.sirspeedyatlanta.com
John Griffies
john@sirspeedyatlanta.com
404-699-0600
Fax: 404-699-0670

Stanton Publication Services
http://www.bookmobile.com
Margit Ahmann, Customer Service Representative
mahmann@bookmobile.com

763-398-0030
Fax: 763-398-0198

Starnet Digital Publishing
http://www.starnetdp.com
Karen Crusius, VP of Sales
karen@starnetdp.com
309-664-6444

Tikatok
http://www.tikatok.com
help@tikatok.com
617-297-2859

Town and Country Reprographics,
http://www.reporgraphic.com
Victor Stoykovich, Vice President
victor@reprographic.com
603-226-2828
Fax: 603-225-8437

Trafford Publishing*
http://www.trafford.com
Form: http://www.trafford.com/ContactUs/default.aspx
Toll-Free: 888-232-4444

Tri-State Litho
http://www.tristatelitho.com
Frank Campagna, Vice President of Sales

graphics@tristatelitho.com
800-836-7581
Fax: 845-331-1571

UBuildaBook
http://www.buildabook.com
Ann Levin
ann@ubuildabook.com
866-909-3003

Universal Publishers*
http://www.universal-publishers.com
Form: http://www.universal-publishers.com/contact.php
Fax: 561-750-6797

VBW Publishing*
http://www.virtualbookworm.com
Form: http://www.virtualbookworm.com/contact.html
877-376-4955

Westview Publishing Co., Inc*
http://www.publishedbywestview.com
Mary Catherine Nelson
mcn@publishedbywestview.com
615-646-6134
Fax: 615-662-0946

Wheat Mark*
http://www.wheatmark.com

Sam Henrie
shenrie@wheatmark.com
888-934-0888
Fax: 520-903-1135

WinePress Publishing*
http://www.winepresspub.com
Form: http://www.winepresspub.com/home/contact.asp
360-802-9758
Fax: 360-802-9992

WingSpan Publishing*
http://www.wingspanpress.com
info@wingspanpress.com
866-735-3782

Worthy Shorts
http://www.worthyshorts.com
privatepress@worthyshorts.com

The Writer's Collective
http://www.writerscollective.org
Lisa Grant, Executive Director
lgrant@writerscollective.org
206-984-0313

Wyatt-MacKenzie Publishing*
http://www.wymacpublishing.com
info@wymacpublishing.com

541-964-3314
FAX: 541-964-3315

Xlibris*
http://www.xlibris.com
publishtoday@xlibris.com
888-795-4274
Fax: 610-915-0294

Xulon Press*
http://www.xulon.com
866-381-2665

Yorkshire Publishing
http://www.yorkshirepublishing.com
Todd Rutherford, Vice President
todd.rutherford@yorkshirepublishing.com
918-394-2665
Fax: 918-622-8871

Appendix XIII

Use This Waiver for

Long Citations

Obtaining release forms in advance, and filing them in a safe place, is just another way you can prove to potential publishers that you are a forward-thinking, squeaky-clean, hard-working author who is not going to disappoint them.

The following release and waiver form is formatted with all the proper legalese. Personalize it to fit your needs.

Again, if in doubt, get legal advice.

Release & Waiver Form for the Book

[Your Title Here]

I understand that [Name of Publisher] (henceforth called the "Publisher") will publish a book tentatively titled [Your Title] (hereinafter called "the Book"). The Book will be written by [Authors Name(s) Here] (henceforth "the Author").

In consideration of the possibility of some portion of [content description type here including words like: my life's story, my photograph, my poem, as applicable] appearing in the Book, I (input your name here) _____ hereby give and grant to Publisher,

Author and their representatives permission to use my name, original content and image in whole or in part, in the Book and subsequently in any media form, and for any purpose whatsoever in connection with the Book, including, but not limited to serial rights before and after publication of the Book, dramatic and non-dramatic performing rights, public reading rights, sound reproducing and recording rights (including but not limited to audio recordings, television, satellite, cable, and radio broadcasting), CD-ROM interactive and electronic rights (including but not limited to Internet, podcasting, and cell phone network), multi-media, motion picture rights, foreign translations, curriculum products, magazine articles, printed excerpts and quotes, lyric rights, publishing uses, all forms of adaptations for commercial use, and advertising and promotion.

I acknowledge that Author is the owner of the Book and all uses and rights thereto for all purposes, and that I have no rights to the Book. Furthermore, I shall have no right to receive any compensation or consideration for any uses of the Book or any other work derived from the Book. Nothing herein obligates Publisher or Author to use any of the rights granted herein.

If I provide a photograph of myself to Publisher, I warrant that I have the necessary rights to the photograph to grant the rights herein.

I expressly release Publisher and Author from any and all claims arising out of the use of my name, original content, and photo for the uses granted herein, including but not limited to claims of invasion, defamation, and infringement of the right of publicity.

This Agreement will be governed by the laws of the state of [Your State]. Venue for any disputes arising hereunder shall be at [Your] County, [Your State]. This Agreement shall be binding upon and inure to the benefit of the successors and assigns of both parties.

Executed on _____ (date), at _____ (city and state).

_____ (Signature)
_____ (Print name)

Mailing Address

_____

_____

IF THIS RELEASE AND WAIVER IS SIGNED BY SOMEONE UNDER THE AGE OF 18, THE FOLLOWING MUST BE COMPLETED AND SIGNED:

The undersigned hereby warrants that I am the parent or legal guardian of the above person, and have full authority to authorize the above Release and Waiver, which I have read and approved. Further, I hereby release and agree to indemnify Publisher and Author from and against any and all liability arising out of the exercise of the rights granted by the above Release and Waiver.

Signature: _____

Print Name: _____

Address: _____

Date: _____

Appendix XIV

Obtain a www.YourName.com

Why should you have a www.YourName.com?

Having a unique URL (www.YourName.com) is almost as important as having a telephone number. Business cards, postcards, handouts and emails should all include this easy-to-remember Internet address. Promoting your book without a website is practically unthinkable. Still, it is possible that you simply do not have the money or knowledge to design an entire site right now. If this is your situation, go with the easy, inexpensive and fast URL forwarding option described below.

Why register IMMEDIATELY for a web name?

Over 1.7 billion people worldwide have access to the Internet (1) and this number continues to grow. URL's (www.YourName.com) are like gold. The longer you wait, the more picked over the gold mine will be when you get there.

Secure your URL as soon as you can, even if you don't have the money or inclination to build a website any time in the foreseeable future. Keep reading and take this minimal action now.

What good is a URL without a website?

Many people start by purchasing their URL and having it forwarded to an existing site, for example, an Amazon book promo page. I first learned about this option when working with speakers at my site, http://www.womenspeakers.com.

They purchased their URL, added it to their publicity pieces, having it forward to their personal speaker profile at WomenSpeakers.com. Later, when they could afford it, they had a website designed. At that point, a small coding tweak sent guests to their new site.

How do I register and forward a URL to my Amazon book page now?

The steps to this process are not difficult, but need to be taken in the order given.

A. Choose a web hosting service that will "forward" your web site.

- I use http://www.godaddy.com
- Another popular site is http://www.gator.com
- Review 10 top hosting site options here: http://www.webhostingchoice.com/

B. Search until you find a name that will work for you. Names to consider are:

- Your own name (SharonMcKenzie.com)
- Your book title (SharonShares.com)
- Your publishing company name (SharonsBooks.com)
- Your name plus a verb (SharonWrites.com)
- Your name plus an underscore (Sharon_McKenzie.com)

Keep hunting until you find the URL that you will enjoy using hundreds of times over the years, on the radio, from stages and in your writing.

C. Register your domain name by following the directions provided at your host site.

D. Select the FORWARD option and send guests to your book promotion page at www.Amazon.com.

Note: To find your own "link," go to your book promotion page. In the address bar at the top of the screen, you will see your URL. For example, the eBook version of the resource you are currently reading is located at:

http://www.amazon.com/eBooks-Idea-Amazon-Days-ebook/dp/B003552LHC/ref=sr_1_1?ie=UTF8&s=digital-text&qid=1263944071&sr=8-1

You must copy your own URL exactly, all of it, or it will not work. As soon as it is set up, guests who type in http://www.YourName.com will immediately see the page to which they have been forwarded.

End Notes

(1) http://www.internetworldstats.com/stats.htm. September 30, 2009

Appendix XV

Outsource Virtual Assistants

As I mentioned, I love working with outsourcers and freelance providers. I depend on them.

The following is my philosophy for this aspect of my life which. I hope it might help you if you are new to the concept of hiring outsourcers.

1. Select, register with and learn to quickly navigate your way around one or more outsourcing sites.
2. Search for providers using very tight, advanced search options to eliminate the need to "reject" numerous unqualified candidates.
3. Determine your minimum requirements. Depending on the scope of work, my minimum standards include: excellent English, 5-star ranking from previous employers, at least six months membership at the site, activity within the past few weeks.
4. If I need the project done in tandem (them working at their desk while I am sitting at mine), I opt for outsourcers who live within a few time zones of my own. If work times are irrelevant or less important, I find excellent outsourcers from nations all over the globe with the added advantage of radically lower hourly rates.

My goal is to find and partner with candidates who have a great reputation, whose price point matches my ability to pay, and with whom I may be able to establish a long-term relationship, despite the distance.

In an effort to build that type of rapport, I think of them like my other employees, each of whom brings value to my life. My outsourcers bring their skills, availability and willingness to work. In return, I am grateful. I pay them their requested wages and, to the best of my ability, treat them like I would like to be treated if the roles were reversed.

After much research, the only two outsourcing sites I want to mention to you.

- ODesk at http://www.ODesk.com
- Elance at http://www.Elance.com

This section is included because most Americans have never hired an outsourcer, even though many have toyed with the idea or at least heard of it.

I like outsourcing: It is not safe, but it's fun.

By "not safe," I don't mean that I feel endangered when working with outsourcers. I do, however, face the fact that my outsourcers do not behave like my American team. For example:

- My local employees get a schedule and either show up or find a sub whereas my outsourcers work when they work and often cancel or postpone after making a commitment to work.

- My employees view their position with our companies as stable and long-term: we have a very low turnover rate. My outsourcers come and go. I cease to need the one service they provide, or they get other jobs, quit or are terminated by me.

- My employees feel like family, and even when they move, or start homeschooling their kids, or go off to college, we still see each other and keep in touch in a casual way. When I lose an outsourcer, they are truly gone from my life and I miss them.

Cultural Differences Create Challenges

There was a traumatic day a while ago when I was keenly aware that I had outsourced my website programming.

I logged in one morning to find a bug in the system that shut everything down. My sites get thousands of hits a day, so it is a big deal if they go down.

Skyping my contact in India, I alerted him to the problem and asked for assistance. He got right on it. After a while he let me know that they would have to build a code to clean up the files. (We have over 2000 pages and multiple sites.)

I was relieved at the progress until I got the next message, which read, "I am going home now. Is there anything else you need?"

It was at that moment that the full weight of cross-cultural outsourcing hit me. My mom had been a programmer for years before she retired, and if there was a big problem, she'd work through the night.

In the end, I would choose to use outsourcers again, despite the occasional hiccup. The beautiful site at http://www.WomenSpeakers.com would still be only a dream if not for these less-expensive, skilled and available programmers from abroad.

Your Play-by-Play Game Re-Cap

The following document includes the actual conversations I had with the eight outsourcers who made this project possible. We removed their names and intentionally did not include any of the U.S. freelance providers mentioned in this section.

An outsourcer works from within a parent company which exists to connect them with clients. As mentioned earlier, I recommend ODesk or Elance.

Free-lance providers are entrepreneurs who work independently of a parent company. The ones included in the appendices of this book have their own websites which clearly define their areas of expertise.

Americans are comfortable with free-lancers like babysitters, lawn care companies and lawyers. But outsourcers are a whole new ball game and I include this section to help the curious get a sneak peek into the highs and lows of hiring assistants sight unseen.

As you proceed to read the communiqués, please understand our formatting and goals. It took my assistant, Kari, hours and hours to copy and paste the inclusions, but that is exactly what she did: Copy and paste.

One other note before we begin. I usually go with lower priced Virtual Assistants. If they charge more than $10 an hour, I'm going to hire a local Personal Assistant, for sure. I did spring for a few higher priced VAs and freelancers for certain aspects of this project, but my experience to date indicates that paying more doesn't always mean getting better quality.

A few technical notes:

- All conversations, even the sad ones, are included for your scrutiny.
- This is an honest account of how this project went down, including the typos, slang, and grammatical mistakes.
- The names of the outsourcers were removed, as many have full time jobs they do not want jeopardized.
- Any financial conversations are indicated with $$.
- Some comments have time notations and some don't. The idea to capture the text came later in the progress at which point some of the time-logs had already been submerged. We copied/pasted the information in the order presented.
- We "piled" each message into one continuous flow, unless it included bullet points.
- All attachments and eBook content (which had been pasted into messages) was removed to reduce clutter.

My goal is to show you a model for working with outsourcers. Other people probably dance circles around me, but I have hired about 30, so am getting the hang of it. I am definitely still learning with every single experience.

Note: Below you see actual, transcribed word-for-word, conversations between myself and the outsourcers hired from either Elance or ODesk. All typos, improper usage and other errors are retained intentionally, to give you a real feel for what it was like for me to work with outsourcers and for them to work with unedited me.

Thursday, Jan 10, 2010
Posted a New Request for "Researcher"
I need this easy research project done asap. If you are available TODAY, keep reading!
Goal: Find me articles from FREE services like ezinearticle.com on the topic:
How to write and publish your own eBook.
I need a simple list under each category including:
a) article title and
b) article URL
for at least 5, preferably 10 articles under each category listing:
1 - How to Format an eBook
2 - How to Add a table of contents to your eBook
3 - How to add an appendix to your eBook
4 - How to add graphics to your eBook
5 - How to convert your eBook from word to .pdf/eBook format
6 - How to upload your eBook to a sales site
Article requirements:
1) It has REAL, instructional content vs. sending me to a sales page.
2) It has at least one list - lists are GREAT!
An example of the ideal article is this one:
http://ezinearticles.com/?How-to-Publish-Your-Book-Digitally-on-Kindle&id=32505734
The example has my "dreamlist" inclusion:
4) It has an author with a pro photo and a website.
Plus: A list of any "free eBooks" on the subject that you stumble upon as you research.
Deadline: Monday, 1/11.

Communiqués with Hired Researcher, Provider A
Note: This one is really long, but important. Very educational for me.

Thurs, Jan 7, 2010
From Provider A
Hi Marnie, So long the info you want is available can find it for you by Monday morning 10.00hrs, am your time, is that ok with you? Thanks Provider A

11:11PM-from Marnie
Hi, You may go ahead. Just do your best. I do feel this is a much easier task than the last. I personally could find SO much, just ran out of time to do it all myself. Thanks! Marnie
PS - It wouldn't let me hire you for that job and keep the previous one open. Is it OK to just pay you $$ from the old job posting when you're done with this project? It would save me time and be the same $$ for you. Thanks! Marnie

Sat, Jan 9, 2010
From Marnie
I will be out now until early Monday. I hope you are progressing well. I think I have more work this week - on this same project. Do you have any availability? Just checking, because I'm not sure yet. Thanks! Marnie

From Provider A
Yes im available, if you are out early morning, can i deliver late monday evening or any other day you prefer. May i ask, is it another set of categories for $$? if yes, thats great.

Mon, Jan 11, 2010
From Marnie
Do I have you working on anything right now? Do you have time to find me 10 article URLs on "how to host a blog tour for your book"? I just need URLs, only. $$ for this. Thanks! Marnie

From Provider A

Marnie, i sent you this email, i coulld not find relevant articles on appendix(you can minus this from the payment or give me another). I done the rest, plzz have a look and if you are ok then you can make the payment. After this i can do the next one for $$.
Thanks Provider A (attachment)

From Provider A
Marnie, despite spending so much time, i could not find info/articles on adding appendix to word/eBook, except for microsoft online guide. Out of 6, i have done 5 categories, i have also find close/near in cases where i cld not find the perfect one. Awaiting your feedback. Provider A(attachment)

From Marnie
OK - I already paid you $$ to you for the "how to format an e.doc project... right?
Did you want $$ more? Confused. I do need you to find me 10 article URLs on "how to host a blog tour for your book"? I just need URLs, only. $$ for this. Thanks! Marnie

From Provider A
No you did not pay me, i just checked my records, when you make a payment i get a messg from [provider], i sent you doc on the urls, you did not approve of ceratin ones, so i modified and put in new info. I was to deliver on Monday, wc i did, You used the old job posting. to hire me. As per my [provider] records i have not received any payment for the e-book creation. Thanks. ps this is final one of all urls for eBook wc i sent to you yesterday.(attachment)

Tue, Jan 12, 2010
From Marnie
I am on chat with them right now. Something is wrong with how it is reading my CCard. Please keep working for me... I

am working to get you that payment to you right now. Sorry for the confusion! Marnie

From Marnie
OK - It's done. Shew! Do not fear that I will not pay you. I love your work and am happy to have you on my team. Thanks for working hard! Marnie

8:15 AM-from Provider A
Marnie, I got the payment thanks, i love working for you, dont wory, i will start on the next assign for $$ tmorrow and if you have more assignments i cna do them.
Thanks Provider A

From Marnie
I am thinking 1 hour = $$ ($$ take home for you). So give me your best shot at getting this done and I will be happy to pay you up to $$ for today.
1 Provide a list of 10 URLs with a photo of an "editor for hire." Here I am looking for high-end, big buck editors whose profiles are not inside a service like Odesk/Elance. You may wish to start with the following task, as links for these types of services should be easy to find as you progress.
2 - With all the rest of your time, find me as many "how to write/publish an eBook" BLOGS as you can that are operated by individuals vs. invisible people. I am seriously hoping for over 100. Include in a Word.doc:
- URL
- Contact email
- Name of the prominent person
- Link to their blog, if they have one

These are everywhere and should be no problem to find. Your time will be consumed finding, copying and pasting the contact information, but I need it. I am counting on you! This part of the research is absolutely critical and I

have no one else assigned to it. Please do your best!
Thanks! Have a GREAT day! Marnie

9:45 AM – from Provider A
I just finished the 10 article urls, actually i have put 13, found extras, Thanks

10:13 AM – from Marnie
Awesome. What is your availability during the next 24 hours? I have more work.
1) Are you finishing up anything for me (I have lost track!)?
2) Are you free to take on more?
3) If so, about how many hours do you have?
I have projects of differing lengths, all due very soon!

10:37 AM – from Provider A
im confused here? for $$, you want 10 urls and over 100 blog links, mmmmm thats a lot, i may not be able to do 100. i will try my best,

Wed, Jan 13, 2010
12:42 AM – from Provider A
Since it night here, i need at least 24hrs to do the assignment, time is 24.00hrs tuesday night. I can do it tomorrow ie wednesday so by wednesday late morning i can deliver depending on workload.
1) i've finished all the work
2) yes im free
3) as many hrs needed,

2:17 AM – from Marnie
I will send you some work. Sleep well!

3:16 AM-from Marnie
Hi Provider A, I am just checking in - It's the middle of the night for me, but want to make sure you are OK and proceeding. Actually, for $$, I want 10 hours of your work. I

am hoping that allows you to get me the 10 editors for hire PLUS as many eBook how-to blogs as possible, up to 100. If you invest less than 10 hours, please just tell me how many hours you worked and I will pay $$/hour, which translates into $$/hour, which is more than you charge. I hope this makes sense. Thank you!!!!

3:26 AM-from Marnie
OK - I'm heading back to bed. Just needed to feel sure that were able to proceed. (Ie- I had paid you, you understood the tasks, etc) Thanks for all your help always, and especially this busy week!

5:55 AM-from Provider A
Marnie, then it would be a hourly job..... i would prefer to deliver a certain amount of work for said amount of money. is that not ok with you? I can try to reach 100 target plus the 10 editors. What do you say? Thanks Provider A

6:01-from Marnie
if you insist that's what you want then I can.....

7:46-from Marnie
I am rather desperate right now, so yes. Please immediately send me as much as you have done now. I need to start using it right away. Send the rest before you sign off for the day. Thanks! Marnie

9:43 AM-from Provider A
Marnie, i have been working like crazy, i just finished the 10 urls part 1 of the project. Will do the 2nd part ie hopefully 100 urls or close to. Provider A

9:44 AM-from Marnie
Great! You go, girl!

9:50 AM-from Marnie

ok will do, maybe i may be able to do a 100 today itself, it s 21.30hrs pm here, i think i can do half and rest tmorrow is that ok with u? Thanks Provider A

10:02 AM-from Provider A
little confused here in 2nd part u asked for how to write eBook blogs right? yet the info u asked for is:
url
email
name
link (is not the same as above url) when its a blog

10:09 AM-from Provider A
some blogs are people, actual but they dont give email id, only form to fill yet i can see their photo

10:13 AM-from Marnie
Ok. Forms are ok but e-mails are better. Say, did you mean to send me a file with the 1st project? Marnie

10:27 AM-from Provider A
oops sorry i thought i sent u. here it is, (attachment)

10:34 AM-from Provider A
could i send you part 2 by tomorrow morning ur time?

10:43 AM-from Marnie
No. My deadline is tonight. Please send me what you have done. Marnie

10:43-from Provider A
i will send in an hours time

10:51 AM-from Marnie
No. I need them within about 4 hours. The job ends now. I have to get the book to the editor by morning. They are

useless to me past midday my time. Thank you for trying. Anything you have completed would be helpful

10:58 AM-from Provider A
so far i ve got 3 links, will do as much as possible say 50 ok?

11:00 AM-from Marnie
Thank you.

11:31AM-from Provider A
i ve done the first 10, will send more (attachment)

12:23 PM-from Provider A
its midnight, i searched for hrs, i know u said the info is easy to find, but actually its not that easy, i ve used all serahc engines to look, msn,bing,ask,google,yahoo. and i have come up with 22. im really sorry.

12:31 PM-from Marnie
Thank you for doing your best. I will give you a good ranking. Good night.

Wed, Jan 13, 2010
11:38 PM-from Provider A
Marnie, I am sorry if i ve dissapointed you, i mean you ended the assignment with me. plzz tell me is that why you are ending the assignment. Provider A

11:43 PM-from Provider A
Marnie, i just gave a feedback, actually i wanted to give 5 but its come as 4.7, im contacting [provider], and trying to modify that Thanks Provider A

Thu, Jan 14, 2010

4:52 AM-from Marnie

Dear Provider A, You provided me with very good research this past month. But, you are correct, I am disappointed in you, but possibly not for the reason you guess. It became very clear to me yesterday that you were charging me much more than your published hourly fee for the work you were submitting. Other researchers were also submitting work, and you were getting paid 2-3x their wages for the same quantity of research. It is possible, of course, that your research skills are simply less developed than theirs, but that also seemed unfair, because they were charging less per hour than your published rate. So, earlier this week, I asked if we could switch your pay to hourly, so I could further assess the situation. You declined. Yesterday, I felt it would be in my best interest to end the work order with you and to use a provider with whom I felt I was being charged fairly. To be honest, I hope you can reconsider your earlier decision and allow me to pay you hourly for an hours' honest work --- because I really like you! I like your work, your personality, your promptness and I would like to continue working together, but only if it can be good for both of us. Let me know what you think. Love,
Marnie

10:00 AM-from Provider A
Marnie, I understand your disappointment, you actually told me that you would give $$ per link thats how we started. I have seen many providers getting so much less then they deserve for a lot of work. I dont think im being dishonest, then buyers can be dishonest too when they expect a lot of work for peanuts. I am one year old on [provider]. I too like working with you but you are implying that im being dishonest, if you had frankly told me this before ending the assignment, we could reached an agreement. I am here to make a living too. Thanks Provider A

10:04AM-from Marnie

I'm sorry if I hurt you. I was telling you my honest feelings: I "felt" like you were being dishonest. Previously, upon first having that feeling, I offered to move you to hourly, which would have provided your required wage. Your negative response to that reinforced my "feeling." Then, yesterday, when you were able send, was it 22 links, in such a short time, but I had contracted for a large sum, I again "felt" the situation was unfair, especially compared with the production of other researchers. Thus, it is maybe best for us to now be done. I'm sorry. I am sad to end the work with you. You did a good job for me. All the best in your future!
Marnie

Post a Job for "Researcher"

Thu, Jan 7, 2010

Are you fast and available immediately?
Find me at least 10 URLs of seller's sites where eBook authors can upload their eBook and be paid for their work: FOR SALE sites like Kindle™ https://dtp.amazon.com/

The above IS the job.

Secondary: Along the way, keep a list of all the sites you run upon where authors can upload their eBook and have it given away: Sites like http://www.free-eBooks.net/submissionForm.php

These do not count in the 15, but this list will be longer than the main one.

Communiqués with Hired Researcher, Provider B

Thu, Jan 7, 2010
From Provider B

Hi Marnie, I have been associated with internet-research and data-compilation related jobs over the past five years. Currently i am working for a British online directory as a copywriter through [provider]. I am also working full-time with a media-monitoring company as an abstract writer for Australian finance dailies. If you give me a brief walk-through about the project, i can get on with the work. I was wondering if you could make this job an ongoing one instead of a fixed one! (I am available 8 am to 11 am your time - CST)
Thanks for considering me. Regards, Provider B

From Marnie
I have no time to further explain the job. If you are unclear, please ask me a direct question. I also will not change the payment for this job. I have no time to do so. If your work meets my requirements, I will consider doing future assignments as fixed. I will hire you now. You may begin immediately. If you are VERY unsure, please submit 3 URLs to learn if they are what I seek. Thank you. Marnie

Fri, Jan 8, 2010
8:14AM-from Provider B
Hello, Are these the type of websites you are looking for? [Provided 2 examples.]
Regards, Provider B

9:12 AM-from Marnie
Hi Provider B, Thank you for checking in. No, these are not what I am seeking. I need sites where a completed eBook can be uploaded, by the author, so that others can buy that

eBook from the URL provided to me, like Amazon.com. The sites you provided help the author create the eBook, but don't actually "sell" completed eBooks. Please
reply with another example asap. Thank you! Marnie

9:41AM-from Provider B

1. Sample 1......**No**

2. Sample 2....**Yes**

3. Sample 3...**No**

4. Sample 4.......**No**

5. Sample 5.....**Yes**

Are the above true? Thanks, Provider B

9:58 AM-from Marnie
Perfect! Exactly what I'm looking for. Go fast until you have 10 yes's and you're done.
Re: 5... that link didn't work for me. Thanks, Provider B. I like you already! Marnie

10:49 AM-from Provider B
Hello, Please have a look at a few more and advise. Thanks, Provider B (attachment)

10:54 AM-from Marnie
Perfect. Just add a "free" or "sell" and sort them to have the "eBooks for sale" sites show up first. As soon as there are 10 of the for sale sites, you're done. I'm very pleased! Marnie

11:57 AM-from Provider B
Hope the second list on the spread sheet helps, too. Thanks for being so considerate.
Regards, Provider B (Attachment)

1:08 PM-from Marnie

You Rock! Way to go, Provider B! Sweet! OK - I am HAPPY to pay you for this project. Now, I have a question. How much do you charge per hour? I am going to hit odds and ends (2 min, 5 min) research tasks for the next 5 days. I can wait up to 24 hours for a response. Interested? Marnie

1:32 PM-from Provider B
Hi Marnie, I leave it upon you to decide. Thanks, Provider B

Mon, Jan 11, 2010
From Marnie
Two more research categories to add.... Hey, Can you do all this in 24 hours?!
If not, tell me and I'll assign these last 2 to someone else! 1. How can your librarian help you research and write your book or eBook? 5-10 URLs 2. Why should a writer join a local writer's club? 5-10 URLs

From Provider B
I believe i can carry out the assignment in totality. I can work for 2 hours today and continue with this work from 2 am up to 11 am CDT. Thanks, Provider B

From Marnie
Perfect! Do it!

From Provider B
Thanks. But you need to hire me first.

Tue, Jan 12, 2010
From Marnie
You are hired... cannot believe I failed to do that; well, I can. The hours are rushing by at the moment. Thanks, Provider B! Let me know when you have anything for me! Marnie

From Marnie
Critical research for today: - 20 of the top eBook-writing experts and coaches.... I need their names, website URLs and contact emails. - List of 10 URLs for people (like Joshua at http://www.eBookArchitects.com who will help you format and upload your Word.doc somewhere online as an eBook. I do not want outsourcers listed in sites like Odesk or Elance, instead, sites like Joshua's that are professional looking and provide eBook formatting services for itunes, Kindle™, etc.
- Find 5 URLS each for sites like http://www.essayrater.com and paperrater.com that provide "auto" editing services for free or low cost.
- 5 URLs for webwizards that help you create a bibliography like EasyBib.com (http://www.easybib.com - 10 URLs for individuals (again, not Elance-type sites) like http://duncanlong.com/art.html that provide graphic art services for authors/book covers.
Wish list if you have any time left: - 5 URLs for sites where you can join a writer's club online. (Don't take too long, I don't know if these exist.) - What are some other keyword search tools besides Google's? Just search, "Keyword tools" or the like. Maybe 5 or 10 including the name of the service and the website. - Total count of books by author, Kathleen Krull. - How many pages long is The Great Gatsby? - Number of website hits that Amazon gets per day. - How many pages does a book need to have in order to have a spine? I know that books with less than 100 pages don't have spines. Gosh! I sure hope you can work today or I'm toast! Thanks, Provider B! I'm so grateful!
Marnie

2:13 AM-from Provider B
Hi Marnie, While I concur that it is appropriate to communicate through email, i also reckon interacting via IM would speed things up. You are the best judge though.

10:49AM-from Provider B
Hi Marnie, Is this OK? Regards, Provider B (attachment)

10:58AM-from Marnie
You are a rock star!!!!! I love it! Please reply, do you have any additional availability during the next 24 hours?
Thanks Marnie

11:12 AM-from Provider B
Hello, My regular night shift (media-monitoring) starts in a few moments from now.
After some rest in the morning, i will be available for more work. (2 am - 11 am your time). I do not have night shifts on Fridays and Saturdays; so i can stretch a bit more on this project on Fridays, Saturdays and Sundays. Indian Standard Time is about 11.30 hours ahead of the Central Standard Time. Many thanks, Provider B

11:17AM-from Marnie
Perfect! I will send any remaining research before then. The majority must be done by tomorrow, so this will be our last "push" day. After that, I will may small projects from time to time, but nothing like this. I just want you to know how to plan. You are great to work with. Love it! Marnie

Wed Jan 13, 2010

8:48 AM-from Provider B
Hello Marnie, Is this the kind we are looking for: [sample]
Thanks, Provider B

9:08 AM-from Marnie
yep - more like that

10:41 AM-from Provider B
Hi Marnie, I will not format the data henceforth, while presenting it in Word. Hope these are OK. I am sorry I

could not find more tools for 'Online free editing services'. Most websites that i came across required the user to download their software. Should i continue with the remaining work tomorrow? Regards, Provider B

10:45 AM-from Marnie
No. Thank you so much. We are out of time now. Thank you, Provider B! You've been awesome!!

10:52 AM-from Provider B
Thanks for the appreciation. Regards, Provider B

Posted Job for "Editor"
I need a 100 page eBook completely edited on Fri-Sun, Jan 16-18. I expect LOTS of red ink, but need an editor who take my final rough draft word.doc and correct every grammer & phraseology error and typo FAST.

Communique with Provider C

Fri, Jan 8, 2010
From Marnie
Hi Provider C, I think I am interested in hiring you for this position. The work needs to be done next weekend Friday, Jan 15 - Sun, Jan 17. How many hours do you estimate it will take? If you are free this weekend/week, you could give me an hour estimate on editing the eBook here: http://www.sanesns.com/eBook.pdf If that one could get edited, that would be so helpful to me and we could see if you and I are a good fit. Let me know! Marnie

From Provider C
Hello Marnie, My apologies for the delay in replying! I estimate that editing an eBook of approximately 100 pages, if it is similar to the eBook you have linked to, would take me between five and seven hours to edit. It may take me

less time, but I feel that five to seven hours is a safe bet. An hour estimate for the eBook you have linked to is between one and two hours. Would you like me to edit it and send it back in PDF format? By the way, question about editing... You sent the eBook in PDF format, but if something needs to be changed, is there a Word document in which the content can be changed? In a PDF format, the best I can do is leave many red comments and arrows to inform you of grammatical errors, etc. Sincerely, Provider C

From Provider C
Hello Marnie, I just finished the edits on the PDF in red. I hope that you will find the comments helpful. It was a very interesting article: I had to return to several pages for proofreading because I became so absorbed in reading the content! Please let me know if there is anything else that you need assistance with. Sincerely, Provider C

Sat, Jan 09, 2010
From Marnie
Super! Wow! How long did it take you? Also, please send me the direct link to your page.

From Provider C
Hello Marnie, [profile page link] Sincerely, Provider C

Sun, Jan 10, 2010
From Provider C
Hello Marnie, My apologies for the delay in replying! I finished the editing in 2 hours exactly. Sincerely, Provider C

From Provider C
Hello Marnie, I declined the offer somewhat unintentionally. I was attempting to make a counter offer and didn't see an option, but I thought that there might be a way to change the terms through declining the offer. The

only thing that I would like to change is my hourly wage. I do not think that it is particularly fair to you for my hourly wage to be $$. I would prefer to work for $$ hourly on the project. I would be able to edit your eBook on Friday any time between noon and 9PM my time. "Please forward me a copy of the edited eBook to [email]" The edited eBook you are referring to is the PDF file with red comments that I sent you over [provider], correct? I will be sending you this copy through email as instructed. Thank you for your time and I am truly sorry for the trouble I may have put you through in (unintentionally) declining the offer! Sincerely, Provider C

Mon, Jan 11, 2010
From Marnie
Hey, will you do the time conversion for me? I am in the Chicago, US time zone

From Provider C
Hello Marnie, I am actually also in the U.S. There is a one hour time difference between Chicago and here. Therefore, in your time zone, I am available for work between 11AM and 8PM on Friday. Sincerely, Provider C

From Marnie
Well, I am so excited: You are WAY the editor for me!
1 - Don't forget to bill me 2 hours for the SANE project.

2 - Block off your schedule to do the main editing job this Friday.

3 - Do you have availability today/tomorrow?

I need the following, but, if you can't, please reply ASAP so I can hire someone else. Thanks! TASK 2: Open the attached "12 Keys" document and select the most important 5-7 questions under each of the 12 headings. Do not select questions that seem outdated or redundant. Send me a new

document, formatted the same as my original, but with your revised version. TASK 2: This one is harder. I need you to log into both my [provider] and Email accounts. [I will change both passwords before you enter and after you finish, so there will be no vulnerability for either of us.] 1. At [provider]: I need you to copy and paste the text from every work order and conversation between me and potential/hired outsourcers beginning January 5, 2010. 2. In my Email Account: I need you to copy and paste every conversation contained in the file named "AA - EBook Project." Compile these work orders and conversations as follows:
1) One section per person or business.
2) Under that heading, include the work order or invitation to work 1st.
3) Follow that with each conversation in the order they occurred.
4) Edit each work order and conversation and make needed corrections to grammar and spelling only. Do not change my use of words or jargon.
Notes:
- Use only first names: Do not show last names, emails, website links, etc.
- Use Arial, 12 point font, single spaced with a 6 pt. spread
- Lay out the document in simple, non-table, format, using the best possible indentation for this type of content
Return this to me ASAP. Oh, I hope you can do this! That would be awesome! Have a super day! Marnie PS - Thank you for catching the $$ thing. It had bothered me, because it was so much different than what I first wrote down. (attachment)

From Provider C

Hello Marnie, TASK 1: I have some time today, but if I don't finish this editing job by tonight due to other appointments, I will be able to finish it tomorrow. TASK 2: I do not think that I would be able to do this given my skillset; I am not a

Personal Assistant. Unfortunately, I believe that you will have to find another provider to do this task for you. I'm not even sure that this task is within [provider's] terms and conditions. You're welcome. I forgot that my provider profile rate was set at $$ and I wasn't sure whether you had noticed or not. Thank you for hiring me and I look forward to working with you. Sincerely, Provider C

From Provider C
Hello Marnie, Here's the finished product for Task 1. Let me know if anything needs to be changed. Sincerely, Provider C (attachment)

12:03 AM-from Provider C Alarie
Hello Marnie, Here is the edited eBook that you requested sent to this email address. I hope this is what you were looking for. Sincerely, Provider C (attachment)

Wed, Jan 13, 2010
From Marnie
Hi Provider C, I am just checking to be sure you are still reserving Friday all day for my book editing project. So I can plan appropriately, please reply with which of the following types of editing are you planning to do? 1. Proofreader: Identify and correct typos, punctuation, misspelled words and inconsistencies in formatting. These can all be accomplished with an online editing tool as was described early. 2. Copy Editing: Proofs for all of the above plus identifies errors in capitalization, word usage and tone. 3. Full Scale Editors (sometimes called Hard, Heavy, Developmental or Substantive), edit for overall congruity. They report on your book's readability, believability and consistency. They look for red flags, unnecessary repetition, cumbersome phraseology and other writing death traps. 4. Formatting Editors tackle the nuts and bolts like page margins, line spacing, indentation consistency, endnotes, heading sizes, references and citations. 5. Technical editors

are fact-checkers, whistle blowers and the ones who can spot an exaggeration a mile away. They test everything from recipes to computer codes so readers do not get stuck with a failure when attempting a described process. So excited to have you on board! Thanks! Marnie One last question: Do you have experience creating bibliographies? That is a job that needs to get started today, and I don't have a provider. Just curious. Thanks! Marnie

From Provider C
Hello Marnie, Sorry for the delayed response! I shall respond to your message in the order that each point was stated. Yes, I still have Friday and Saturday reserved for your eBook editing project. I do not work on Sundays, but I do not anticipate that a third will be necessary to complete the editing necessary. The types of editing that I intend to be responsible for in your eBook are proofreading, copy editing, and full scale editing. However, I can also work on formatting and technical editing if it is deemed necessary. Yes, I have had to create bibliographies and works cited pages on several occasions for research papers. I will probably be able to fit your project into tonight's schedule. What is the bibliography page for, do you have the sources/books/websites for me to cite? What citation style would you prefer (MLA, APA, etc.)? Are parentheticals or footnotes/endnotes included in the work that you need the bibliography page for? Sincerely, Provider C

From Marnie
Hi Provider C, Thank you for you reply. I ended up subbing for an employee at the restaurant and just returned home now. 1) I will have the final, rough draft eBook to you by Friday morning. What time is the earliest you could start work on it? (Every minute matters on this project!) 2) I am excited about the breadth of your editing and look forward to your input. 3) The biblio is coming along, so that's ok. 4) Re: Tonight. are you still available? If so, could we chat on

the phone a few minutes? I'd like to explore the options that are open to me for tonight... if you are still free. If not, no problem!
Thank you so much. Marnie Good night

8:37 PM-from Provider C
The earliest time that I can start on Friday is probably 10AM my time, or 9AM your time. I am sorry that I could not respond sooner. Do you have Skype and would you be available to chat sometime tomorrow? Tomorrow I have an appointment with someone on Skype from 6-8AM (your time), but any time afterwards I will most likely be free to chat. Thank you! Sincerely, Provider C

Thu, Jan 14, 2010
From Marnie
Hi Provider C, I'm at [phone number] or you can give me your number and I'll call you.
But honestly, I'm not sure we need to speak: I am just hoping that you might be able to let me send you an early, very rough draft of the final manuscript this morning. I want the "global" editing done today so you can focus on the proofreading, editing, formatting and technical editing tomorrow. My PA, Kari, is also going to read it this morning to answer the questions: 1. Does this make sense? 2. Where do I get lost or confused? 3. Does a certain word, phrase or concept get overused? 4. Is the process comprehensible? 5. Does anything about my writing cause you to dislike me or question my motives? 6. Would you recommend this book to a friend? 7. If you were a budding author, would you consider buying it? I could have it to you by 10 AM. Let me know! Marnie

1:35 PM-from Provider C
Hi Marnie, My apologies for the delay! I overslept this morning and have just finished checking emails now. I believe that I will have some free time today to work on

editing, so feel free to send me what you have so far. Thanks! Sincerely, Provider C

2:52 PM-from Marnie
Super! That's Great! I am attaching the pre-rough draft version and I am going to CHANGE my request. Since I need this back by 7 PM CT, please accomplish the following list as far as you get, but in this order. You can finish everything else tomorrow. Notes:
- XX means the information is still to be added
- the Bibliography is being built
- Kari is editing from ch 6- appendixes as I type for "clueless" readers who know nothing about the topic. When I submit it to you by 10 AM CT tomorrow, all the XX's (excepting the formatting pages/etc) will be done and her changes will be made. To prepare it for me to do my final draft tonight, please use these minutes to:
1) Format the indented lists using the correct examples on page 10 and 18 as your guide. For some reason, my Word.doc kept making different list notations despite every effort to fix that.
2) Spacing is driving me nuts. I think I'm closer now, but if you could get that fixed today, I'd be so much happier reading it tonight.
I need the edited copy back into my email bin no later than 7 PM so I can spend all night finishing it up. I will not work on it again until I receive your revised copy, so don't let me down! So excited to be working with YOU!!! God speed! Marnie
Oh - It's too big to attach, you may view it online here: [online link] Gotta go - My radio talk show starts in 8 minutes. Yikes!

6:04 PM-from Marnie
Hi Provider C, I hope you have had a chance to work on this at least some. Please send it to me at [email] when you are

ready now. Please stay online until I indicate that it has arrived to me. Thanks! Have a great night! Marnie

7:08 PM-from Provider C
Hi Marnie, I hope the file size wasn't too big. Let me know if there are still formatting errors... I think there was one in the Table of Contents, but other than that, up until page 21, I haven't seen anything. Would you like me to continue working on this tonight or wait for instructions in the morning? Sincerely, Provider C

9:27 PM-from Marnie
No No Wait until morning. Thanks

11:45 PM-from Provider C
Hi Marnie, Slight problem. I believe that I told you my hours of availability tomorrow were 9AM CT until 7PM CT. A teacher at my alma mater has given me and another person last minute notice that she would like us to visit to do a science demonstration for all of her classes. This results in a change in my availability to 10AM-11AM CT (offline), 2PM-9PM CT(online), and any time after 10PM CT(online). I also have availability on Saturday, though I am unsure exactly what hours I will be available that day. I hope that this does not present a problem. If there are no additions or significant changes for pages 1-20, I will probably be able to finish the editing in a timely manner tomorrow. Sincerely, Provider C

Fri, Jan 14, 2010
10:09 AM-from Marnie
Hi Provider C, OK. I am counting you to give this your full attention for many hours. I hope you can. 2-9 tonight can work. In fact, ideally, if you send me your results at 9 tonight, I could make my changes and let you do a full scale, final read-through for any final edits we have missed. How would that be? This HUGE project is resting on your

availability to complete the editing on time and well. So please, please, for both of our sakes, find a way to give this your undivided attention for several hours. I am counting on you! Thanks! Marnie

10:22 AM-from Provider C
Hi Marnie, Those were my available hours for you. I intend to devote all of that time to working on your editing project. I might be able to work on your project sooner as it seems that the person with whom I am volunteering with is not ready to go yet. Right now, however, I am working on writing two articles for another buyer because the deadline is today. That's fine; I will get the edits to you for 9 tonight so that we can do a final read-through then. Thank you! Sincerely, Provider C

11:43 AM-From Marnie
Super! Sounds great.

Post Job for "Brainstorming"

January 13, 2010 [Note: I hired 3 outsourcers for this job.]
need help with this one thing today. It has to be done on January 13th, the earlier in the day, the better. The title of the eBook is: EBooks: Your Ticket from Unknown Author to Amazon in Seven Simple Steps Below is my rough draft titles for my table of contents. It needs help!! I would like you to send me a list of alternative chapter titles.
Give it your full attention for as long as you can for $$ (one logged-in hour) and be as zany, humorous, serious, whatever, but reply with several alternative ways to describe what will be found in each of these chapter in 10 words of less each.
Preface: How the book, "eBooks," went from Idea to Amazon in 13 Days

1 – Now is the Time to Publish Your eBook, don't wait, a window of opportunity to publish now
2 – How to Make Your Writing Irresistible to Publishers, why you want to keep focusing on the traditional houses while writing for the eBook market
3 – Keep It Legal, no plagiarism, etc.
4 – How to Write Your Book for eBook Distribution, making it work in eBook format
5 – Hire an Editor - why editing is critical to your success
6 – PDF, Mobi Pocket & ePub, understanding your eBook upload options
7 – Don't Flirt with Failure, prepare to succeed by taking preventive action before you post to AMazon
How I dissected®Appendix XX – Writing: The Marnie Method this project and how you can use my method to write your next book
Appendix XX – How to work with PAs, VAs and other outsourcers - includes actual time tables and correspondence logs as examples of what a working relationship looks like
Appendix XX – Expert Advice from a Kindle™ Guru - Chapter by Joshua Tallent
Appendix XX – Sample Questions Editors Must Ask - Chapter by Kathleen Krull
Appendix XX - Templates - how for format your documents in advance to save time and money
Appendix XX – Citation Samples - how to format your bibliography as you go, to save time and money

Communique with "Brainstorming", Provider D

Thu, Jan 13, 2010
From Provider D Marnie--I wish you had interviewed me before you hired me for this job. I am buried in work right now and couldn't even look at this material until end of next week. That's the life of a freelancer. Their workload

can change in an instant. I am going to have to cancel this job, but perhaps we can work together on future projects! Hope so! Thank you for thinking of me. Provider D.

From Marnie
I am so sorry! Actually, it didn't even occur to me to worry about it, but I wonder now - does it reflect badly on you if I hire you and then you do no work for me? I'm so sorry! I just didn't know. Marnie

From Marnie
Hi, Marnie! No, it does not reflect badly on me, nor does it reflect badly on you! It's the nature of freelancing, which is at the heart of [provider].

Buyers post assignments and hope many freelancers will apply so they have a good selection of skills and fees from which to choose. But freelancers have to apply for lots of jobs, usually, to snare just one. There are no committments or guarantees bt Buyers in any assignments posted on [provider] when, in fact, the Buyer will hire someone. Sometimes Buyers just let the job posting expire after 30 days without hiring anyone at all!

Conversely, freelancers cannot guarantee their availablity beyond the moment they apply for a job. Often hours, or even minutes, before someone wants to hire a particular freelancer, someone else does first. Also, to further complicate matters, jobs sometimes take longer than both Buyer and Provider anticipate or they end more quickly. It's an iffy situation but it's just the nature of freelancing.

People who deal with freelancers all the time, like magazine editors, always ask first, "Do you have the time to...?" do a particular assignment because they know it's a "catch as catch can" situation.

The best route to take for both parties is to have an interview before the hiring decision is made. That way you, the Buyer, know the actual availability of the Provider, and both you and the Provider have a clearer understanding of the scope and time required to complete the work.

Hope this helps! Please keep me in mind for future projects! Provider D

Communique with "Brainstorming", Provider E

Thu, Jan 13, 2010
From Provider E
Dear Ms. Swedberg, My ideas are attached below. Hope they are useful! Sincerely, Provider E [attachment]

From Marnie
Smashing! You rock! Thank you, thank you!!

From Provider E
You are welcome! :)

Communique with Provider F

Jan 13, 2010
From Provider F
Thanks for the hire and the note.
I can definitely fit you in today, that's not a problem. I'm not sure exactly when yet, but I will have it done for you today; I just need to massage my schedule first.

From Provider F
Just in case you didn't get my email: I'm sending you the file here. [attachment]

Post Job for "Research Assistant"

Are you fast and available immediately? Find me at least 10 URLs of seller's sites where eBook authors can upload their eBook and be paid for their work: FOR SALE sites like Kindle™ https://dtp.amazon.com/

The above IS the job. Secondary: Along the way, keep a list of all the sites you run upon where authors can upload their eBook and have it given away: Sites like http://www.free-eBooks.net/submissionForm.php These do not count in the 15, but this list will be longer than the main one.

Communique with Research Assistant, Provider G

Thu, Jan 7, 2010
From Provider G
Dear Ma'am, Thank you for considering me for this position. For 10 years of work experience, I was able to develop a strong expertise in data entry, data collection, internet researching, article submission, documentation and very proficient in MS Office applications(Word, Excel, Powerpoint, Outlook), Internet Explorer, Mozilla Firefox, Google & SAP applications. I was given the opportunity to work with different kind of projects in [provider] as a Personal/Executive Assistant, Internet Researcher, Web Marketer, Editor/Proofreader, Customer/Email Support, Project Manager, Data entry specialist, & Forum Poster/Blogger. As a Personal/Virtual Assistant, I do research projects, data entry, transcription, myspace sending messages, article submission, web marketing, compose correspondence/reports, & administrative management. I have an excellent English skills and able to present the project in the most appealing and exciting manner possible. I'm a hardworking, reliable, internet-savvy & passionate person. I always strive for continued excellence in my work & I'm willing to learn quickly to the job assigned to me. I always do my job with

professionalism, integrity, 100% accuracy & customer satisfaction. I am willing to dedicate myself on a long-term basis. I have proven multi-tasking capabilities with strong ability to plan, prioritize and manage complex projects under aggressive timelines. I am a team player, hardworking and results-oriented. With excellent interpersonal & organizational skills and can relate well with all levels in an organization. I can be reached online daily through Skype(Provider F.santillan) or Yahoo Messenger(ayen_santillan) GMT+8 timezone and I always check my emails 24/7. I believe that my rate is competitively fair based on my knowledge & skills that I have gained from my previous work experiences. Looking forward to hear from you. Thank you & Best regards,
Provider G

Fri, Jan 8, 2010
From Marnie
Let's get going! Here is the job: Find me at least 10 URLs of seller's sites where eBook authors can upload their eBook and be paid for their work: FOR SALE sites like Kindle™ https://dtp.amazon.com/ That IS the job. 10 for-sale sites for eBook authors as described above.
Secondary: Along the way, keep a list of all the sites you run upon where authors can upload their eBook and have it given away: Sites like http://www.free-eBooks.net/submissionForm.php
These do not count in the 10, but this list will be longer than the main one.

Sat, Jan 9, 2010
From Marnie
Provider G, STOP! Please stop you work on this project as it has been completed by another researcher. Please reply with the data you have already collected, if any.

If you would like 5 stars for this task, please advise me of how many hours remain available for my use of your researching skills for a different project. If you don't mind taking a lesser rating, just submit any data you collected, stopping at this point, and we'll call it done. Please do let me know. This was my error, but I would like to have something to show for the $$, if possible. Thanks! Marnie

Jan 10, 2010
From Provider G
Hi Marnie, Will it be possible if you can give a new project instead? I think I still have 3 days with the schedule. I didnt realize I have other teammates working in the same task. Thanks, Provider G

From Marnie
Sure! That'd be so helpful for me. I actually made a mistake and hired two of you for the same task. Thanks for being flexible! Researcher - Provider F
- 40 total links: 10 links for each chapter to online news/ezine/other articles by unique authors - Requirements: o Author must have their own website link to a http://www.yourname.com (NOT http://www.xxx.com/xxx/xxx/... Links must end at .com/.org) - Task: Create a word.doc (not excel) with o Chapter title followed by 10 individual article 1) titles, 2) ULR of article, 3) author name, 4) author link I will be traveling all day Monday, but will check my email before I leave in 10 hours from now. If ?? - send them asap. Thanks! Also, if you will not be able to complete this task today, please reply so I can find another provider for this one. There is much to be done in a tiny window. Thanks!

Mon, Jan 11, 2010
From Marnie
How is this coming? I need this ASAP.... really. Thanks!

No further communication.

I hope this section has been helpful in giving you a taste of the vast difference between VAs. You will notice that my writing skills improve with time, attention and editing, and that I could have handled the situation with Provider A better than I did. If I had it to do again, I would establish clear boundaries instead of throwing out accusations while frustrated. I believe it is a hard balance to keep both parties happy when either feels they are being unfairly treated.

Appendix XVI

Promote Via Blog Tours

Scheduling a blog tour before finishing your manuscript is a bit suicidal. I am feeling that pain today, but convinced it will be OK.

A blog tour is like a book signing tour, except you don't leave home, you don't sign books and you don't usually sell too many books, but it gets the chatter going.

Just like with a physical book event, you schedule guest appearances at several other people's blogs during a certain time frame. You secure a date, submitting pre-typed answers to their questions or provide a blog post or pre-selected segments from your book.

On the day in question, you show up to greet the guests and reply to their comments and questions. It is a virtual rendition of a live promotional event.

This appendix is divided into two sections:
1. Blog Tour Tips I Learned Along the Way.
2. Blog Tour Host Companies to Consider.

1. Blog Tour Tips I Learned Along the Way

As part of the research I did for my own life-journey as well as this book, I engaged a firm called Pump Up Your Promotion to "model" a blog tour for me. I selected a 5-day, 7-site tour and invested less than $200. I will tell you that Dorothy was like a little Energizer bunny, and I totally got my money's worth!

Between what I learned from watching her work (via emails), and what I gleaned by reading dozens of "how-to's" on the topic, I can give the following input:

- Prepare your basic package early: 1) Book cover .jpg, 2) your photo .jpg, 3) Title, Subtitle, ISBN details, 4) Book summary (short and long), 5) Author bio (short and long), 6) social networking links, 7) your book promo page and "buy me" links, 8) favorite excerpts you will provide.

- Create a separate email account to receive update notifications from blog tour sites. Check it daily during pre- and post-tour weeks and multiple times daily during your tour. Be prepared to visit the sites several times on the actual day of your post, and a few times during the following weeks.

- Start a calendar for this project. I use SuperSaas for all my projects, media interviews and other booking needs. My affiliate link is: http://www.supersaas.com/?af=4087-Marnie. Jan Faber is the designer and this time-saving system which is taking the world by storm. He predicts that within a few years, you will no longer call a receptionist to make your dental or doctor's appointments... you'll be visiting a site like SuperSaas. I highly recommend it.

- Research to find blogs that address readers in your genre. It doesn't really pay to post on a site for pet lovers if your book is about Ancient Greece.
- Contact potential blog hosts as early as possible. I had only 3 weeks notice, so many opportunities were ruled out based on timing alone.
- Expect to give a free copy of your book to each host and to have a drawing for a free giveaway daily, from those who register at your blog tour pages.
- Be willing to answer questions or write a guest post on their choice of topics (that relate to your book). If given a word limit, honor it.
- Set up your tour so people can know where you have been and where you are going next.
- Use your newsletter, blog and social networking connections to get the word out. Brag up your blog tour hosts.
- Do a press release announcing your tour, including dates and stops.
- Change the links on your main page the day after each post, so your permanent blog link takes futures guests to your promo page within a blog instead of to the front page (where daily-breaking content dominates attention).
- Send prizes to the winners and include their names in a prominent place on your blog tour site.
- Send each host a thank you note or gift. Ask your hosts to provide positive feedback at Amazon or somewhere else.

Note: Many tour guides require hosts to submit statistics following a guest appearance. This is optional. When organizing my own blog appearances, I did not do this.

I have learned to never despise the small things. Numbers are important, but I can tell you from personal experience that just one guest has the potential to change the trajectory of a project, career or life. Value each hit, each comment, each host as if it was the most important connection you will ever make.

PS – I like to apply this same principle when meeting people on the street or at our business, restaurant or church. Each person is valuable, regardless of their ability to "pay you back" for any kindness tendered.

----

2. Blog Tour Host Companies to Consider

I engaged this company to model a pro blog tour for me: Pump Up Your Promotion

http://virtualbooktours.wordpress.com/

Here are additional options for consideration and comparison:

Blog Stop Book Tours
http://blogstopbooktours.wordpress.com/

Christian Speaker Services
http://www.christianspeakerservices.com/css_blogtours.htm

Kidz Book Buzz
http://www.kidzbookbuzz.com/

Latino Book Tours

http://www.latinobooktours.com

Promo 101 Virtual Blog Tours
http://virtualblogtour.blogspot.com/

PrPr
http://www.prpr.net

TLC Book Tours
http://www.tlcbooktours.com/

Appendix XVII

Prepare Yourself for

Common Questions

This section is included to give you an inside peek into the type of questions you can expect to be asked should you choose to pursue a blog tour or any other type of media interview. I've included my answers for your entertainment.

Q. Give a short description of your book.

A. *eBooks: Idea to Amazon in 14 Days* is ideal for how-to and business authors who want to take their words from private to public.

Did you know that you can now publish your training materials, employee handbooks, or new how-to resources right onto Amazon within a matter of days? You don't need an agent or publisher and the price is right.

This book reads like a personal journal, but it is actually a guide for any author who is ready to see their book being sold on Amazon.com this week, this month or this year.

The blow-by-blow progression of Marnie's 2-week journey, from idea to publication, provides step-by-steps, shortcuts and success strategies. Increased interest in eBooks and handheld readers is turning the publishing world upside down. Now is the time for you to take action.

Q. Does your book have a handle?

A. Sure! It's the book that enables any author to get onto Amazon in a matter of days.

Q. Who will enjoy this book?

A. Every person who has a concept, idea or story in their head that they want to share with others will find value in this training. Basically, as of today, anyone, including you, can take your concept, create a manuscript and put it up for sale at Amazon.com as an eBook, a paperback or both.

Q. Are there other books on this topic? How does yours differ?

A. There are a few, but the topic and contents of the book are changing by the hour. This is definitely the up-to-the-minute resource for authors who are serious about getting onto Amazon.

Q. Why are you the right person to write this book?

A. I didn't choose myself. A regional library directory chose me as the right person as the author of 10 books and eBooks, a pinch hit trainer, and a library lover. Once chosen, I invested every ounce of energy and every resource I could muster to put together the best training on the topic available right now. I hope I succeeded.

Q. What are your three favorite reviews so far?

A. David Sanford, a literary agent, wrote, *"Make 2010 the year you write and sell your first eBook. Marnie's fast-paced book tells you virtually everything you need to know. Highly recommended!"* Melissa Smallwood, a professional organizer, wrote, *"Inspirational! After reading Marnie's book, I am ready to write! The information is extensive, well organized and includes everything a writer needs to achieve the goal of becoming a published author."* Gail McKenzie of the Quantum Team wrote, *"An amazing resource: a useful, easy to read, easy to follow guide for anyone who is looking for guidance in the EBook arena."*

Q. If you could choose any way to promote your book, how would you do it?

A. I love radio talk show interviews: I enjoy being interviewed, but I also benefit from interviewing others, so I host my own weekly show.

Q. Why are you doing a virtual book tour?

A. I believe in the power of the web. I am actually promoting public libraries during National Library Month's "Read Me" Week. As part of that project, I am supporting authors through a live training program this week called, "PRO Author Training" available via Marnie.com. My book is the vehicle which allows me to promote the other two opportunities, and this blog tour is one of the ways I am getting the word out.

Q, I understand that you are touring with Pump Up Your Book Promotion from February 22-26 via a virtual book tour. How did you choose these dates and what do you hope to accomplish?

A. I am promoting National Library Month and, specifically, "Read Me" Week. My book came as a result of being contracted by a regional library system to do a 3-day, 7-city tour. I was hired to train authors how to write eBooks. I decided to model the behavior, and here we are. I'm getting the word out about this training. It all just seemed to fit together.

Q. What do you hope to communicate during this virtual book tour?

A. I especially hope to encourage new or unpublished authors to take action now. There has never been a better time to get published. My book explains how I did it in 14 days. Anybody can do this!

Q. What do you think about offline book signings? Do you have preference-- online or offline and can you give us the reasons why?

A. Oh, gosh, I hate offline book signings. I always ask to do a presentation or a demonstration, but never just a signing. It's awkward. Having said that, I will add that we host author book signings at our espresso café; they have their place, and some authors love them, but I don't like them at all.

Q. How did you decide you wanted to be a writer? Were there any authors or books that made you think "Wow, that's what I want to do - craft stories of my own for others to read"?

A. I was never going to be a writer, just an entrepreneur. But people started asking me how I did "food". I was entertaining over 100 guests per month, serving great meals and spending less than $.50 a meal per person. I interlibrary loaned over 200 books, trying to find just one that explained my kitchen shortcuts. That experience changed my life: I could not find a single book describing the food processes I used. What I did find was less than inspirational: many of the books I reviewed during that process were poorly written. I remember thinking, "I could do better than this."

Q. What made you take that leap from wanting to be a writer, to actually becoming a writer?

A. I only write when I need to. For example, I never wrote books about home management or homeschooling because there were other books on those topics that said everything I wanted to say, and they said it better. I take on new writing projects the moment I realize that what I have in my head has not yet been communicated, shared clearly or taught inspirationally. Answering people's questions, so long as they are within my scope of understanding, is something I love to do and it motivates me to write.

Q. Are you married or single? Do you have kids?

A. Definitely married! Dave is a great guy and we've been together 26 years. We have three awesome young adult kids. We will be empty-nesters next fall when our youngest, Timothy, heads off for college.

Q. How do you combine the writing life with home life?

A. I almost always write in the night: it's the only time I can be uninterrupted. I try to be accessible to family and employees during the day and sometimes I succeed. It's never easy to find time to write.

Q. Do you have any pets?

A. At the moment, we have fish and two dogs, Allie (Poodle/Maltese) and Dallas (Springer Spaniel). We have had dozens of pets through the years—every kind except monkeys and snakes, I'm pretty sure. Our retail store, Soulutions, has a pet department, so we often have "guest pets" including chinchillas, birds and rabbits. It's a zoo around here.

Q. What are you reading right now?

A. I'm always reading about five books at a time. Just now I'm loving *Girl Talk* by Jen Hatmaker. She is a riot! She's a pastor's wife and absolutely hilarious. I interviewed her for my radio show last year and have been a fan ever since. Love this little book about the freedom gained when we are willing to be vulnerable. I am also reading, *Leading with a Limp,* by Dr. Dan Allender. People look to me as a mentor despite my glaring weaknesses and this book is a breath of fresh air in a culture that worships outward perfection.

Q. Who are some of your favorite authors?

A. Shaunti Feldhahn, Nancy Missler. Joyce Meyers. Jan Johnson. Kathleen Krull.

Q. If you could have lunch with any author, dead or alive, who would it be and why?

A. Jesus. I know He didn't write a book, but the Bible describes Him as "The Word" and "The Author and Finisher of all things." So, definitely, a face-to-face with Jesus would be out-of-this-world!

Q. Where do you get your ideas and inspirations?

A. My people are always asking me, "How do you do that?" Every book I've written has been in response to that question. I answer with the appropriate length of response. Often I give a 140 character social networking update, a blog post or an article. Sometimes the question deserves an entire book.

Q. What do you like to do for fun when you're not writing?

A. I love to read and learn. I missed that as a child—because I hated it all so badly then. I think I'm making up for lost time.

Q. Where do you like to vacation?

A. My favorite vacation spots are wherever my family and friends are. No kidding! Location is far less important to me than relationships, although I've been a lot of places and pretty much loved them all.

Q. Describe an ideal vacation.

A. Traveling with my husband, Dave, provides unique rest and reconnection opportunities that I highly value. He usually has more energy than I do on vacations, so my favorite scenario includes him being extremely busy in conferences or something for several hours during the day, while I laze around. Then, when he is finished with his stuff, we go do something fun for the evening.

Q. If you could be anywhere in the world for one hour right now, where would that place be and why?

A. Key West, Florida, on my sister's sailboat, surrounded by my four nephews. It's not about the boat, because I get sea sick. It's about the people. I admit, the weather helps, because it's sub-zero (15 below) as I type.

Q. What's your favorite library and why?

A. For sure, our local Warroad Public Library. It was donated by Mrs. Margaret Marvin and I was on the building committee. It is a stunning, Frank Lloyd Wright design featuring coves, stained glass windows and study nooks. The look and feel of the building are a testimony to the peacefulness of life in a small town and to the elegance and great taste of the Marvin family and their company, Marvin Windows & Doors.

Q. What's your favorite bookstore and why?

A. Soulutions. That's our family's retail store which includes a Christian bookstore. I remember the day the books arrived and I began putting them on the shelves. I kept pulling out books I needed to read. After a few minutes, I had more books in my personal pile than on the shelves. I decided to put them all back and just go grab one when I had time to read.

Q. What are your greatest frustrations and rewards as an author?

A. I think the traditional publishing process can be extremely disheartening. Often after submitting manuscripts, carefully formatted to the publisher's specifications, I did not even receive a rejection notice. That's a big frustration for an author. Most rewarding? Hearing from readers about how something I said, did or shared positively affected their life. That's awesome.

Q. Who is your biggest fan?

A. People are always telling me that *they* are my biggest fan. Restaurant customers say, "You know that I am your best customer, right?!" One of my outsourcers wrote today and said, "I am your biggest fan." But, honestly, there is only one opinion that matters to me. God gave me everything I have. I believe He is pleased with how I am using the gifts He's given. The idea of having God as my biggest fan is a nice thought. I hope it is true.

Q. What's the first thing you notice when you meet someone?

A. This is terrible, but true. Nothing. It's so tragic. I always say, "If you lost weight, cut your hair or shaved your mustache, and I don't notice, don't take it personally!" I wish I noticed stuff, but I just don't. I am terrible at remembering names, faces or details of any kind.

Q. Tell us a secret no one else knows.

A. My life is an open book... I am wracking my brain! I suppose very few people know about my special map. Next to my desk I have this huge world wall map. It has black dots on every continent, indicating where I have mentees around the world. Knowing I am having a positive impact on people in Chicago and China makes me smile.

Q. Have you ever won anything?

A. The first thing I won was a patch for my jeans from a radio station. I was the 5th caller. I remember feeling like I was going to explode, I was so excited. I think that's why I decided never to gamble. I loved that feeling very much and am pretty sure I'd be an addict!

Q. Where's your favorite place to write at home?

A. My computer. I spend WAY lots of time in front of my computer. I'm actually considering purchasing a notebook computer, just so I can face outwards a few hours a day.

Q. Do you have any particular habits that you take part in while writing?

A. I suppose my main oddity is that I meet with my outsourcers in the wee hours of the morning, before they leave for the day. I work with outsourcers from many different countries around the world and 5 or 6 AM is the best time for us to connect.

Q. Could you please tell us about your writing process?

A. I write how-to books, so I start by researching the topic enough to create a list of basic steps. Next, I hire researchers and assign them chapters to research. While they work, I write the basic content for each chapter. Upon receiving the research results, I personally visit hundreds of article-, news- and generic-websites, sorting, scanning, scouring and selecting key concepts and quotes for the book. This part of the journey often results in radical chapter additions, rearrangement and global rethinking. There are many more steps involved, from the graphic art cover to final draft formatting, but the entire project usually feels like drinking from a fire hydrant: super fast and so much to learn.

Q. What kind of research did you do?

A. On this project, time was extremely tight, so I hired researchers to find websites and articles that addressed each chapter heading. Most of the published documents supported my theories and personal experience, but occasionally the research findings required me to change my perspective and learn a new concept from the ground up. I didn't have much time, so this was tough.

Q. What was the hardest part?

A. Finding time. As the owner and manager of a restaurant, retail store, espresso café and several mega websites, it was hard to fit the writing of this book between catering orders, bills, vendors, traveling to buyer's shows, speaking at live engagements, taking a son to college, managing my home and still finding a few hours for some sleep.

Q. What was the most fun about writing your book?

A. The challenge. I love to communicate as a writer, speaker, song writer and trainer, but for me, the challenge of learning something new energizes me. This project, in particular, was a wild ride!

Q. What are you working on right now? What's your WIP (Work in Progress)?

A. *SANE: Social Networking Success in 15 Minutes a Day.* I launched it as an eBook last fall and it took off. I am currently adding stories from successful Social networkers to flesh out a full-length book that will help people understand how to take advantage of the opportunities available in our interactive, 2.0 culture.

Q. What do you hope to accomplish within the next five years?

A. 20 years ago, I could have answered that question, incorrectly. Now I take one day at a time. If you would have told me five years ago that I would now own a retail store, espresso café, or glow-in-the-dark mini golf course, I'd have said, "No way! I'm too busy!" I gave up the goal-setting thing and just live each day to the max, taking full advantage of every opportunity as it flies by.

Q. What's on your to do list today?

A. Oh, my gosh! Do we have time for that here? I've been up since 4:15 and it is now 6:31 AM. My oldest son is home from college for the day and my youngest has the day off school and work. I'll get the restaurant staff rolling about 9 and we'll probably connect as a family for brunch about 11 AM. From noon to 7 PM I'll work the espresso café, finding time in between customers to place a multi-thousand dollar seasonal order (one item at a time) and set up next month's sale plan for our retail store, Soulutions. After I finish, Dave suggested we go out for supper to "the Black Bear" and then I'll sit in the living room and hope that one of the guys will come talk for a while. It usually works. Bedtime will be sweet bliss!

Q. If you had to summarize your life and give it a book title, what would that title be?

A. Super Busy. Actually, I started writing a book by that title last fall. I think I was built to be busy and I love tackling new challenges. In 2002, we bought a restaurant for me to manage, despite the fact I had never worked in a restaurant, even as a waitress. In 2006, we bought a retail store and espresso café, same drill. I don't even drink coffee. My life is fun, fast and always interesting. I like it.

Q. What do you want readers to take away from reading your book?

A. Inspiration and encouragement. Many authors are overwhelmed by the thought of finding a publisher, discouraged by a pile of rejection letters or confused by the long list of publication options. In these pages, I model a journey, from concept to Amazon, in just 14 days. While it may take you twice, or twenty times, as long as it took me, this book proves that you can get published this month or this year. It is a reasonable goal and within the reach of anyone determined to attain it.

Q. Is there anything that you would like to add?

A. I write virtually for real people, with real challenges, who live in a real world. My hope and prayer is that something I say, write, or do will have a positive affect on your life, or at least on your day.

Q. Where can readers get in touch with you? Twitter, Blog, Facebook, etc?

A. My website is my name, Marnie.com. I am "MentorMarnie" at Twitter and Facebook and "MarnieSwedberg" at LinkedIn.

I'd love it for people to keep in touch!

About the Author

Marnie Swedberg is the leadership mentor and online coach to thousands of women from every continent, career path, and religious denomination. She provides practical, innovative and out-of-the-box solutions.

She has been featured in print and on numerous television and radio talk shows, has written several books and eBooks and is an expert author with Ezine Articles as well as a staff writer with *Live Magazine*.

Currently a pinch hit speaker, she has done presentations for large corporations including Honeywell, Prudential, Pillsbury, AT&T and others; for non-profit groups including Chambers of Commerce, Professional Women's Clubs, Public Libraries, Speaker Training Conferences, Women of Today Groups and writers' conferences; and for Christian Women's Retreats plus programs for denominations including Baptists, Catholics, A/G, EFree, Lutherans and many others.

She exudes a passion for life, loves people and has a gift for tackling new challenges. These qualities, combined with her published works, which encompass most topics related to work, home, family, faith and friends, make her an easy and encouraging guest in a variety of settings.

Kudos

"Marnie Swedberg is an incredible entrepreneurial leader with seemingly endless energy that comes from a passion to live life to the fullest. Her influence and impact on others is the result of a desire to be the best she can be and to help others be the best they can be. Marnie is a successful business person, author, speaker and Christian leader, but

more importantly, she is a successful wife, mother and an inspiration and encourager to women all over the world through her various enterprises."

Rev. C. Roger Stacy, Home Missions Director
& Leadership Coach District A/G

"Marnie is a woman on a mission, many missions really. Each one is executed with generosity and professionalism and speaks to the power of positive intention. Her work providing support tools, resources and advice for Women's Ministry can be seen at www.WomenSpeakers.com, but the benefits of her dedication and effort are experienced around the world. You'll feel uplifted and empowered when you spend any amount of time with Marnie."

Linda M. Lopeke, The SMARTSTART Coach

Contact Information

Book a Media Interview
http://www.marnie.com/media.php

Book Marnie to Speak
http://www.PinchHitSpeaker.com

Apply to Join Marnie on the Air
http://www.marnie.com/Show_Guest.pdf

Contact Customer Service
http://www.marnie.com/support.php
877-77-HOW-TO / 877-774-6986

Mail Marnie a Review Copy of Your Book
Gifts of Encouragement, Inc.
306 Elk Street
Warroad, MN 56763

Enjoy Online Resources by this Author

http://www.Marnie.com
Access all published resources, training programs and family updates.

http://www.WomenSpeakers.com
Find your next speaker at the largest Christian Women Speakers Directory in the world. Over 1,000 speakers represented; some near you.

http://www.LeadershipAttitudes.com
Get training via Marnie's interviews with experts.

http://www.BetterThanaDiet.com
Eat with Gratitude via her 31 Daily Bites for Discouraged Dieters

http://www.WomensEvents.info
Find Christian women's events coming to your area.

http://www.IdeasforWomensMinistry.com
Save time with over 30 party and event publicity theme sets.

http://www.BibleStudyExpo.com
Find your next Bible Study via Marnie's interviews with 24 of the most highly recommended book and Bible study authors.

http://www.TheMillionMileClub.com
Get travel advice from other million milers.

Local Brick & Mortars

http://www.SoulutionStore.com

Visit Soulutions for Your Hobby Home & Heart, the Swedberg's variety store featuring: "Over Coffee" espresso café, glow-in-the-dark, indoor mini-golf, a wall of aquariums, quilting fabric and needlecrafts, office and party supplies, a gift shop, Christian bookstore and more. Located in Warroad, MN, just one mile from beautiful Lake of the Woods.

http://www.MKTakeouts.com
Enjoy M & K Takeout's world class pizzas, tacos and subs. "The best pizza I've ever eaten," is how many travelers describe the House Specialty. Former Warroadians claim, "M&K is the first place I stop when I come home for a visit." Located on Highway 11 East, in Warroad, six miles south of the Canadian border.

Made in the USA
Lexington, KY
15 January 2014